Four Points Rambl

Upper Th...
Wiltshire Ramble

Steve Saxton

Four Points Ramble Association

Published by the Four Points Ramble Association, 18, Bullfinch Walk, Manchester M21 7RG. www.fourpointsramble.org.uk

ISBN: 978-0-9555297-6-4

Printed and bound by: DeanPrint Ltd, Cheadle Heath Works, Stockport Road, Stockport SK3 0PR

Cover design by Pauline Gribben.

The drawings and cartoons on pages 5, 56 & 92 are by Peter Field.

The maps and most of the photographs are by the author. Ishbel Saxton took the photograph on p 121. Madeline Hellier took the photographs on pages 128b & 144b. On the Facebook page:
www.facebook.com/pages/Four-Points-Ramble-Association
many colour photographs relating to this book, and others in the series, can be seen.

Tree Planting Slide and *Madge's Maggot* are by the author. All other songs & tunes are traditional or in the public domain. Some chords and arrangements are supplied by Ishbel Saxton and the author; others are traditional or in the public domain.

Also available from the same author and publisher:

Four Points Ramble Book One: Ramble Through West Yorkshire.
Four Points Ramble Book Two: Ramble Past Manchester.
Four Points Ramble Book Three: East Cheshire & North Staffs Ramble.
Four Points Ramble Book Four: Ramble through the Heart of England.
Four Points Ramble Book Five: Northants & Oxfordshire Ramble
Four Points Ramble Book Twenty-Four: Ramble through North Lancashire.

See the website www.fourpointsramble.org.uk (or the Facebook page) for details of the beneficiary charities, which are different from this book. Details are given on the website, and on the Facebook page, of how the books may be purchased online.

Contents

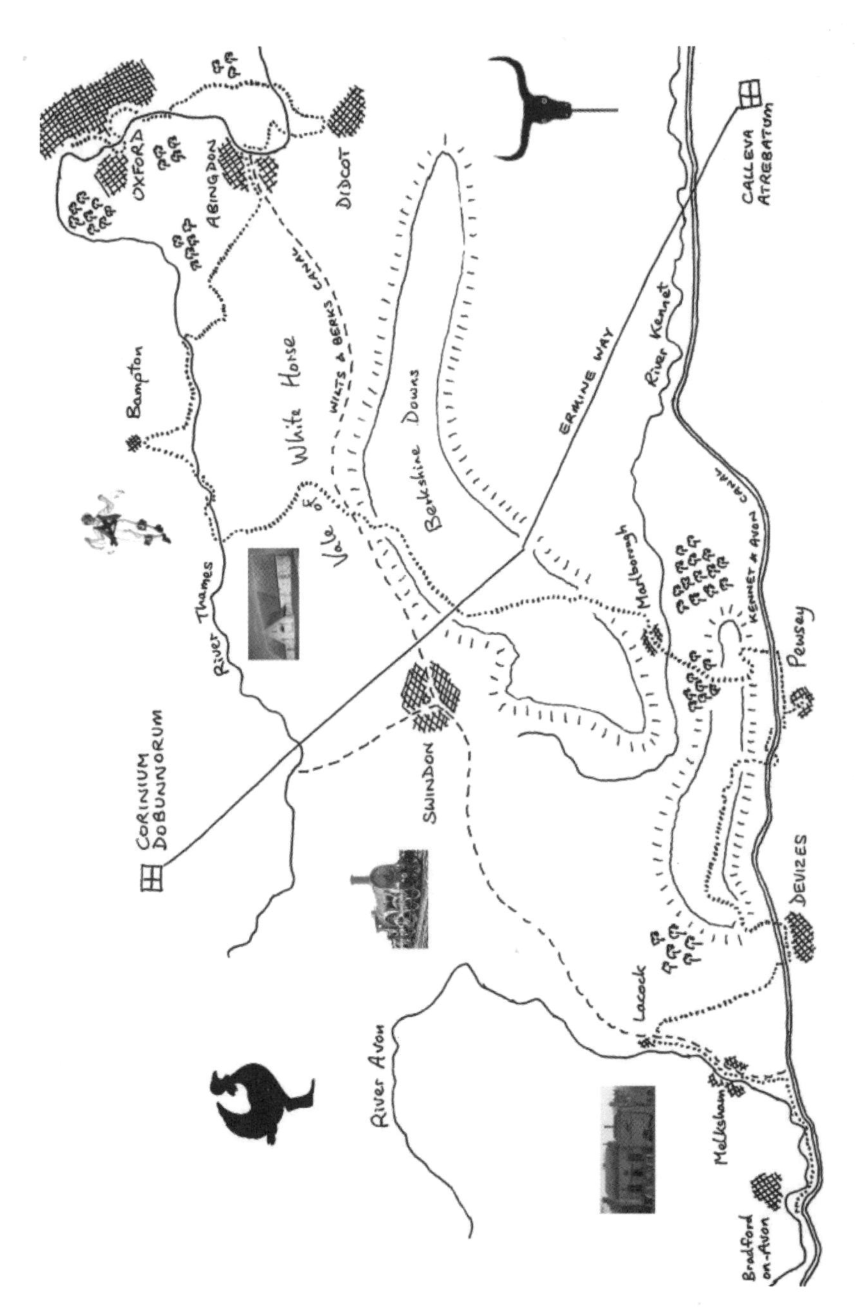

The route of this book

Introduction

One object of this book is to describe part of a geographically, though not chronologically, continuous walk to the four extremities of England: the northernmost, southernmost, westernmost, and easternmost tips of the mainland. This book is the sixth of a series (though the seventh to be completed and published), and it covers a 114-mile section of the journey, in south Oxfordshire and Wiltshire, finishing in Bradford-on-Avon.

The book is a slow travel book rather than a guide book or gazetteer. That is to say, it aims to report on a journey taken, rather than to provide a set of instructions for future walkers. Nevertheless, earlier books in the series have been used as inspiration by walkers following parts of the route, and therefore some topographical details are given, which together with an OS 1:25000 map should make it possible to follow the journey physically, rather than simply in the armchair. In some sections - for example when walking canalside - it is difficult to lose your way; and in others, such as where we follow the Thames Path, guides already exist. But where the reader may be unsure of the route being taken, I try to give adequate directions.

As before, I have indulged my many interests as opportunities have arisen: wildlife, history, literature, music, biography, industrial archaeology (in particular canals and railways in the age of steam), genealogy, heraldry, church history, topography and storytelling.

The route taken may seem curious, for a walker aiming eventually to reach the southern and western tips of Cornwall, sometimes doubling back northwards, but there are reasons for these personal choices that will become clear as the book progresses.

Possible route of the entire project, including sections completed.

One: Wolvercote to Oxford *(3 miles)*

Disappointment – redevelopment – swing bridge – reluctant coalman – forklift – Oxpens Meadow – idle poet – St Scholastica's Day – persecuting the Welsh – Gibbons's Almain

25th October 2011

I set out from St Peter's Wolvercote, the finishing point of Book 5, and walked down the little hill past the Plough Inn. If I hadn't been passing at the very beginning of a walk, it might have been interesting to drop in for some refreshment. Ishbel and I had the chance to look in a few weeks later, to find an interior of much character and considerable age. We settled in the 'library', a room with robust old wooden furniture, a fine bay window, mellow wood panelling and a whole wall of old books. The food was excellent, a class above the average good pub lunch, and I sampled Tolly English Ale, astonishingly light at 2.8%. Even at this low strength, it still tasted like beer, and Greene King are to be applauded for this new venture in reducing alcohol intake.

From the Plough I walked straight on towards Ball's Bridge over the Oxford Canal. The name might have a family connection, for my great-great-great-great-great-great-uncle John Ball was landlord of the Plough at around the time the canal was built in the late eighteenth century.

On Wolvercote Green to the right a large cow bellowed; ahead, a narrowboat glided southwards; but I realised it would pass under the bridge before I got there, and so I would be unable to observe its name and provenance. Nearby, a girl of perhaps six or seven burst into passionate weeping, ran to her mother, who assumed she had been frightened by the volume of the bovine bellow: 'It's only a cow, silly!'

But no: 'I was going to watch the boat, and I couldn't get there in time, and now I won't see it!' The child's interest, and disappointment, had been exactly the same as mine; her violent reaction floodlit the hardening effect of decades of experience. My momentary disappointment had flickered through my mind and vanished, so inured was I to the billion pinpricks of frustrated hopes, plans and intentions, so ready to shrug my shoulders and look for something else to be interested in – such as the wholehearted zest and tender sensibility of a child. We assume that coping with disappointment is a sign of virtuous maturity; but perhaps it simply shows a sad bluntedness, a fading of sharp appetite for the manifold excitement of life.

On the other side of Ball's Bridge was a bigger disappointment: the path onto Port Meadow that I had intended to follow was on the far side of the railway, and there was no sign of the footbridge or tunnel that I had assumed would give access. Most probably there had once been a 'Stop, Look and Listen' crossing at track level, which had been removed in the interests of health and safety.

In the late eighteenth century, an Oxford bandleader noted down a tune called 'Disappointment'; perhaps he wrote it himself.

Disappointment

John Malchair, originally Johann Malscher, was a violinist and music teacher from Cologne who settled in Oxford, and led the band in the Holywell Music Room for more than thirty years, giving up in 1792 when a stray orange, thrown in a student brawl, damaged his Cremona violin. He was an early enthusiast for folk music, noting down airs from itinerant musicians, and his own compositions are very much in the folk tradition.

With no access, Port Meadow would remain unexplored, and I would have to follow the canal towpath, not normally something I would be reluctant to do. But this section of towpath had associations; many years before, I had been trying to walk my way out of gloom alongside the canal, finally admitting to myself that I still loved the girl I had split up with months earlier. They were not memories I wanted to reawaken, but in fact I need not have been concerned. The canal was almost completely unfamiliar; the only view I recognised was the playing fields of the Dragon School. Old memories remained vague recollections, and no more. It was sobering to realise that it was over thirty-eight years since I had walked this way, and quite apart from the fading and fallibility of memory, much had changed. The allotments on the far side of the water had doubtless been allotments then, but the bothy at the water's edge, erected by an allotment tenant who was clearly more interested in fishing than gardening, was more recent.

The towpath was hard and stony, and I was glad of the very tough soles of my old boots – boots that were, as far as I could recollect, forty years old this year. Weeping willows added beauty to the unhurried restfulness of the scene. I caught up the boat that had disappointed the little girl, for it was, very properly, proceeding dead slow past the many moored boats. Part of a hire fleet with a smart blue livery, it was *Cropredy* of Oxfordshire Narrowboats, based miles away in Lower Heyford, at a boatyard I had walked past in Book 5; the family on board presumably had it for the week.

New bridges had been thrown over the canal to give access to new residential developments, and I eventually became disoriented enough to leave the canal a bridge early, at Frenchay instead of Aristotle, on my way to see the house I had lived in in 1973. The mistake gave me the chance to appreciate the Victorian architecture of the small terraced houses on Hayfield Road, clearly now desirable properties. A little further on, I found 16, St Margaret's Road, my former address; though the house did not look as I remembered it. Then, it had been the joint abode of eight postgraduates, two on each floor, and had exhibited the comfortable scruffiness of most such properties; now it was clearly a single household, smartly painted, burglar alarm prominent, the once straggly green front garden now gravelled over (the gravel even matching the cream-washed walls) and occupied by a car no student could afford. I put the camera away; it was the same address, but not the same house, somehow. It was silly to have expected it to remain unchanged over almost four decades, but I had thought that it might still have been the same *sort* of property. Presumably the demand for accommodation within reasonable reach of the city centre had pushed prices up in this area.

I wandered round the corner, wondering if I would recognise Ugu's house in Kingston Road; I didn't remember the number, for I had only lived there for two days. When I first moved to 16, St Margaret's Road (where a friend lived in the attic), I was living in Crispin's room in the basement; he sublet it to me for the Easter vacation. I then heard that Chris on the ground floor was planning to leave for Holland, probably before Crispin's return, so it seemed I could make a seamless transition from subtenant to tenant. However Chris was a vacillator; he could not decide when he was going, or even whether he was going, and in the end I was forced to find other accommodation nearby. As soon as I had done this, Chris made his mind up and left, and I was able to move back, feeling guilty about poor Ugu, a very nice Nigerian gentleman who now had to find himself a tenant all over again. I was also rather irritated with Chris for causing a lot of unnecessary hassle and losing me the cost of two weeks' rent, which was the least I could consider paying Ugu.

Whichever was Ugu's old house, it was also now much better cared for than in the early seventies. I walked on down Southmoor Road, retracing the route I used to walk to work every morning to my warehouseman's job in Osney Mead. Rejoining the canal at Walton Well Bridge, I was shocked at a totally unfamiliar view. A vast and not unattractive redbrick apartment complex spread out on the far side of the canal, while the near side had been cleared and tidied, with a new retaining wall, smart gravel towpath, and neat grass verges.

I struggled to remember any detail of what had been there before; I could only dredge up the vaguest of images of something rather tumbledown, decrepit, and industrial or post-industrial on the far bank, that had loomed over the water; and scrubby trees, maybe elder or hawthorn, shadowing a muddy towpath this side.

The change was in most respects an improvement, if perhaps making the scene a little *too* pristine, neat and tidy; but a few years would soon solve that. I was less disturbed by the transformation than by my inability to form any clear mental picture of the former scene; it was almost as if my past was being taken away. I had to resort to internet research a couple of days later, to establish that what I quarter-remembered was the old Lucy's Eagle Iron Works, which had been built by the canal in 1825, and well suited the old working class terraces of Jericho. However when Jericho became trendy, done up and expensive, the works looked more of an eyesore, and had eventually been replaced by this new development, which promised much more income for the landowners. A little more research provided proof of how upmarket the flats were: £1595 a month for a two bedroom flat. Jericho was certainly climbing the social scale.

A little of the old scruffiness remained further on, as the Castle Mill Stream sidled shadily alongside the canal, one or two tumbledown narrowboats having found their way onto this backwater of the Thames. It had apparently once – long ago – been the main channel, though it must surely have been wider then.

The Jericho boatyard looked much as I remembered it, and the pale Italianate St Barnabas' Church was also unchanged. As I passed, it chimed two o'clock, the chimes curiously soft and thin, almost tinny, and the hour bell light and rather lifeless. John Betjeman thought it a 'nice experience' to hear the tubular bells; I was unimpressed. It was odd, but explicable, that although I had passed the church a hundred times I had never heard the bells before; for my walk to work used to be timed to precision in order to arrive at 7.59, and I knew where I had to be at any given time along the way. So I would always have passed St Barnabas' at exactly the same time each morning, and clearly it had not been at a quarter hour.

A signpost helped me remember the turn to follow the Sheepwash Channel, the short link from the canal to the current main course of the Thames. The path used to run under the railway, and at first I was afraid this quirky footpath had disappeared, for I found myself approaching an obviously brand-new bridge over the Sheepwash into another new residential development. But diagonally opposite, the old alleyway reappeared, skirting round the Rewley Road swing bridge, rusting and ramshackle now, before plunging under the north end of Oxford station, exactly as it had been all those years ago, five feet of headroom with pigeons murmuring right in your ear as you ducked under the girders, the light beyond reflecting off the dark water, maybe a train rumbling close overhead, and a smell of guano and damp feathers.

Rewley Road Swing Bridge, beside which if I remembered rightly (and I might well not) the path had crossed a railway on wooden planking at rail level, had once carried the LNWR line into that company's separate Oxford station. In the mid-nineteenth century, railway rivalries often precluded sensible sharing arrangements, so the LNWR brought its glossy black engines and smart carriages on a parallel track into an ornate station designed on similar lines to the old Crystal Palace. Because the elevation of the line was lower than the GWR, a simple bridge over the Sheepwash Channel would not have given the barges enough clearance; and so Robert Stephenson designed a fine double-track swing bridge.

A hundred years later, in 1951, British Railways finally routed the passenger trains from Bletchley into the GWR station; but the LNWR terminus remained in use as a goods yard, and finally just as a coal yard, until 1984, after which the line was lifted, and the swing bridge locked open and forgotten, to be gradually reclaimed by nature. However there are now moves to preserve the structure, which is unique in certain respects, being largely in original condition and one of the earliest hand-operated swing bridges still in existence.

I had worked from the Rewley Road coalyard for a single day, as a Co-op coal delivery driver's mate. Coal heaving offered a very low basic rate, considering the hard work involved, but there was a tonnage bonus that was supposed to be lucrative. We loaded up in the windswept yard, coaldust eddying all around, my driver lobbing the occasional lump at the blackened scarecrow operating the grab crane (and getting a ferocious oath in return). The driver later alarmed me with his style of one-handed and one-footed driving, his right hand tucked under his thigh, the clutch (and, briefly, the steering wheel) untouched as he changed gear. My foreboding increased as he told me the job was only worthwhile for him because he lived in tied Co-op accommodation at a ridiculously low rent.

I had been nervous of the sacks of coal; but previous heavy jobs had developed the right muscles, and I managed; however, one address having nobody at home, which meant we had to bring many hundredweight back to the yard, drastically reduced our day's total delivery. In the end we had worked over ten hours, with barely a break, and were nowhere near the daily average that would have produced any tonnage bonus at the end of the week.

I decided I had been deliberately misled over the hours and wages, and went in the next morning to ask for my card back (those were still the days when a worker carried a National Insurance card from job to job). The foreman boiled over, claimed the card was elsewhere and could not be retrieved, and vented his rage in a five-minute tongue-lashing which dissected and analysed my character very thoroughly, if not very impartially. I stood and let it wash over me, telling myself it was useful experience (and trying hard not to tremble visibly), and eventually he ran out of breath and pulled the card from a pigeonhole and flung it scornfully on the counter.

It took a little nerve to go back and ask for my day's wages at the end of the week, but I got paid, albeit the bare minimum.

Beyond the hunched-over walk under the railway, the path joined the Thames proper, at a watery crossroads known as the Four Streams. Here there had once been a popular bathing spot, Tumbling Bay, the name suggesting the antics of bold water-fit youngsters. An arched wooden footbridge took the Thames Path over the Sheepwash Channel and behind terraced houses towards Osney. I was delighted by the blue flowers of chicory on the riverbank, especially where they contrasted fetchingly with the bright purple of knapweed.

At the Botley Road the bridge (apparently with the lowest headroom on the entire navigable Thames) was too low for the path to go under, and pedestrians had to come up to the roadside and cross through heavy traffic. Looking for a crossing point, I realised I was almost next to the Youth Hostel, and since it was just after two, I could check in and avoid carrying the rucksack for the rest of the day. Unfortunately I had picked a bad moment, for there was only one person at reception, and I was behind a mature and persistent Australian lady who seemed to have monumental complications with her booking. I stood and waited, wearing what I hoped was an expression of saintly and stoical patience, but it was difficult to forget how far I was planning to go, and how relatively little daylight remained. Eventually, ten minutes after they would have been useful, two more staff appeared and quickly cleared the queue.

The rucksack was soon dumped and I returned in relief to the Thames Path through Osney, past Osney Lock, built in 1790 by prisoners from Oxford Castle. Here *Cropredy*, having negotiated Isis Lock and overtaken me, was now descending with the aid of the lock-keeper. I admired the latter's cabin as I passed; full of smartly-varnished wood, it presented a most nautical aspect. From the basin below the lock, where the Osney Ditch, yet another of Oxford's many waterways, joined the Thames, a tug pulled a heavy commercial barge downriver.

Over to the left, beyond Osney lock, was the site of Osney Abbey, once a powerful institution with a magnificent church. 'It was for 400 years,' wrote Hilaire Belloc, 'the principal building upon the upper river, catching the eye from miles away up by Eynsham meadows and forming a noble gate to the University town.' But the abbey was so thoroughly despoiled at the Dissolution that nowadays nothing at all remains *in situ*, 'contrariwise, electric works and the slums of a modern town.'[1] Among the few identifiable souvenirs are the bells, acquired by Wolsey for his new Cardinal College, later Christ Church. Osney's bells were famous, 'the noblest peal of bells in the land' in ancient times, according to John Buchan. There was a peal of six, each with their own name, dedicated to a saint or commemorating a sponsor: Douce, Clement, Austin, Hautclere, Gabriel and John. The seventh bell was Thomas, the immense clock bell.

[1] Belloc, H (1907) *The Historic Thames* Dent

Buchan paints an evocative picture of the abbey in its pomp, industry, and serenity: the peace of the cloisters and the sounds and smells of the craftworkers outside, masters of leather and wood, beeswax and stone, silver and gold and iron. The abbey wielded considerable influence and economic power, for the Abbot had charge not just of his own abbey, but of numerous other churches, benefices, lands and buildings. Many university students lived in halls owned by the abbey, and studied in schools which were also Osney Abbey property. In 1439 Abbot Thomas Hokenorton rationalised various isolated properties in Oxford town and erected the Schools of Osney, effectively an early Arts Faculty, a long building with ten lecture halls on two floors. But now the glory of Osney is long gone, and only old pictures recall the 'soaring tower of Osney Great Church.'[1]

Walking on down the Thames Path, I was glad to find the narrow alley leading to Osney Mead, along which I remembered hurrying daily at 7.57 or 7.58, checking my watch at fifty-yard intervals. I generally arrived in time; though there was one week when I was one minute late every morning, and highly put out to find on Friday that the clocking-in machine had been two minutes fast all week. Even a minute's lateness cost you 15 minutes' wages, so I was distinctly out of pocket that week; my boss just said 'you shouldn't cut it so fine,' and I had to admit he had a point.

The industrial estate itself seemed vaguely unfamiliar and different; the buildings were still there, but not quite where I remembered them. Kemp Hall Bindery, where I had worked, had gone and the warehouse now housed a furniture storage firm. There was nothing surprising in that, but what I found disturbing was that my memory of how the buildings had stood in relation to each other was apparently so inaccurate that I had great difficulty assuring myself that this was at least the building I had worked in, if not the same company. I had been on the warehouse side, where finished and bound books were stored ready to be sent out; sometimes I drove a Bedford van on trips out, but what I enjoyed most was driving the forklift truck.

It was a Conveyancer stand-up counterbalanced electric forklift, tall and thin to work in narrow aisles, with a very high reach and tiny castor wheels underneath. The steering wheel had a knob attached so that the operator could spin the wheel rapidly from full lock one way to the other, as you raced round a double right-angled bend between aisles. A primitive overhead cage protected you from falling objects, in case you made a nasty mistake high up. It was great fun to drive once you got used to it. But nothing here woke any buried memories; it was almost as if I had never been here at all, and again I felt distinctly unsettled by the reminder of how slippery and elusive memory is, if you have no way of keeping it fresh.

Rather glumly, I returned to the Thames Path, heading downriver by the route I might have taken after work on a Saturday morning; this seemed more comfortingly familiar, the path running over the Bulstake Stream, and under the railway. Black-headed gulls were screaming with gratuitous raucousness, showing bright red bills and legs, and a whole lot of mallard paddled fast downstream in a neat line astern.

[1] Buchan, J (1931) *The Blanket of the Dark* Hodder & Stoughton

I found my way across Gasworks Bridge and tried to decide between the Mill Stream Walk and Oxpens Meadow as a way forward.

Oxpens Meadow was a grassy open space between tree-lined waterways, a pleasant green lung near the city centre, though not improved by the warehouse-like bulk of the ice rink in one corner. Predictably, the meadow was under threat of development, and I hoped that the Friends of Oxpens Meadow would succeed in their efforts to get it designated as a Town Green. From the Meadow I crossed a busy road and proceeded very uncertainly through the bleak and arid concrete waste behind the Westgate shopping centre; it was a depressingly banal and ugly area to be so close to the centre of a historic city. Though I saw no trace of it, I was walking over the course of the Trill Mill Stream, that had once supplied both the Trill and the Blackfriars Mills. The shopping centre had been built over the old Franciscan Friary; Oxford was once swarming with friars: grey friars, black friars, white friars, and Austin friars ministered and preached to the poor from their friaries around the old city walls.

Beyond the concrete, in Turn Again Lane, a few 18th century cottages had been saved from demolition and restored by the Oxford Preservation Trust. From here I turned up a side street to St Ebbe's church, where Alice Laetitia Weaver, one of my great-grandparents, was christened in 1845. Her father was a painter and decorator, and her mother the daughter of a Scottish innkeeper, whose pub in Kingston Bagpuize I aimed to visit later in the walk. Growing up in Oxford, Alice eventually married Edwin Saxton, son of the Wolvercote blacksmith. Edwin worked as a compositor for the Oxford University Press, and I was told, in awestruck tones, that he was a *Greek* compositor, meaning that he knew enough Greek to set Greek text. This would not necessarily imply that he had flawless classical Greek, but at the very least he was familiar enough with the alphabet not to set letters upside down or sideways.

St Ebbe's had a modest façade, as befitted a Low evangelical church, 'very Low' was Betjeman's comment, who thought nothing worth seeing but the Norman doorway. A hundred yards east was St Aldate's, a street where Betjeman had rooms once, as an undergraduate. The young CS Lewis, then still almost a beginner as a Don, was Betjeman's tutor, and despaired of him: 'very idle'; 'pleased with himself'; 'ignorant and stupid'; 'I don't know what to do with him', were typical frank comments in Lewis's diary, and he was not overjoyed at an invitation to Betjeman's rooms for tea ('a damned nuisance'), though he thought the room itself beautiful.

> The conversation was chiefly about lace curtains, arts-and-crafts (wh. they all dislike), china ornaments, silver versus earthen teapots, architecture, and the strange habits of "Hearties". The best thing was Betjeman's v. curious collection of books…[1]

[1] Lewis CS (1991) *All My Road Before Me: Diary 1922-27* Harper Collins

-- one at least of which Lewis borrowed and enjoyed, so the visit was not entirely pointless. Lewis makes no mention in his diary of Betjeman's teddy bear Archibald, the inspiration for Sebastian Flyte's 'naughty old bear' Aloysius, in Evelyn Waugh's *Brideshead Revisited*.

Betjeman, predictably, found Lewis's work ethic impossible to either sympathise with or emulate, and never completed his degree. He left with a grudge against Oxford University (and Lewis in particular) which still did not eradicate his love for the town – at least the more time-weathered and traditional aspects of it. The modern suburbs he detested, along with the motor industry that caused them to expand.

Turning into Blue Boar Lane, I saw a scene that could have dated from Betjeman's youth; all old stone and flaking black iron railings, with nothing more modern than a lot of bicycles to enhance the view. A little way down the street was the Bear Inn, where I used to like to go for a pie and a pint in days gone by; and where I intended to make a short break for memory's sake.

The interior of the Bear was much as it had been: ancient, cosy and wood-panelled, with a vast collection of representative ties in glass cases. I knew my old school tie was here somewhere, but couldn't remember where, and there were too many (or rather, I lacked the persistence) to locate it afresh. The beer was Fuller's, which was welcome but different; in the old days, as far as I could recall, it had been Morrell's, a very local brewery situated a quarter of a mile away by the Castle Mill Stream. Morrell's Brewery closed in 1998, so there was no way to remember exactly how the beer had tasted, though it had certainly been good.

I wasn't intending to eat at this stage, and anyway the homely pie-and-baked-beans that I had usually eaten in 1973 was no longer on the menu; the available food was much more upmarket than that, running to ingredients such as duck liver, goat's cheese, and tiger prawns. I decided to have some crisps, as something that wouldn't have changed much, but had to smile when the least exotic crisp flavour turned out to be Sea Salt and Cider Vinegar.

Most of the customers in mid-afternoon seemed to be female students, which was another change of atmosphere from the heavily male-dominated university of previous eras. For hundreds of years there had been no question of females studying at Oxford; the pioneers had only arrived as late as 1879; and even then they had had to set up their own colleges. The ancient all-male colleges did not begin to accept women till 1974, just after my fairly brief time in the town.

There is no clear starting point for Oxford as a place of learning; the seeds that would grow into a university were already sprouting by the mid-twelfth century, when Roger Vacarius was lecturing on law and preparing the *Liber Pauperum*, an early legal text book. Students flocked to Oxford, for a time the only place in England where the poor could gain an education and so move up in the world. Then as now, this was sometimes resented by local people, who saw the students as pampered parasites, and there were serious battles between townsmen and scholars.

The most memorable took place in 1354, and started, as such things often do, with a very ordinary incident. On St Scholastica's Day, the 10th February, a group of students entered the Swyndlestock Tavern and called for wine:

> John de Croydon, the Vintner, brought them some, but they disliking it, as it should seem, and he avouching it to be good, several snappish words passed between them. At length the Vintner giving them stubborn and saucy language, they threw the wine and vessel at his head. The Vintner therefore receding with great passion, and aggravating the abuse to those of his family and neighbourhood, several came in, encouraged him not to put up with the abuse, and withal told him they would faithfully stand by him.[1]

From there matters escalated predictably; church bells were rung to summon help: St Martin's to call out the town, and St Mary's to rouse the students; then town and gown attacked each other. On the first day none were killed; but the next day the town arrived in much greater force, and the scholars were set upon in Beaumont Fields. The fighting continued through a third day, and the students had much the worst of it; in the end well over fifty had died, and almost all others had fled.

The town's triumph was brief; the effective destruction of an institution of national importance aroused the wrath of King Edward III, who was actually not far away at Woodstock. He appointed a Commission to inquire into the facts, and the town was placed under an Interdict for two years, which was only lifted on payment of substantial compensation, and the institution of a ceremony of penance: an annual Mass for the souls of the slain, and the symbolic offering of a silver penny from the mayor, the bailiffs, and each of sixty burghers. This annual St Scholastica's Day ceremony was not discontinued until 1825, and for those four and three-quarter centuries it symbolised the hold the university had over the town, who were never allowed to forget who ruled Oxford.

[1] Wood, A, cited in Rashdall, H (1895) *Universities of Europe in the Middle Ages*

While the town thereafter felt too constrained by higher authorities to get involved in fighting, the students were happy to fight amongst themselves, the different 'nations' – Scots, Welsh, Irish, Northerners (ie north of Trent) and Southerners – always ready for hostilities. In 1389 the Welsh were being persecuted by the Northerners:

> And certain persons they slew and others they grievously wounded, and some of the Welshmen who bowed their knees to abjure the town, they the Northern Scholars led to the gates, causing them first to piss on them, and then to kiss the place on which they had pissed.[1]

The expression 'take the piss' is not recorded before the 20th century, but it would appear that taking the piss out of the Welsh, at least, is a much older tradition.

However, the many instances of riots and brawling during the Middle Ages were spread over hundreds of years, and we should not forget that life was normally peaceful, with many opportunities for fun. There were Town Waits (later City Waits, when Oxford gained a cathedral) to play their instruments and entertain the people; William Gibbons was among their number at one stage, and his son Orlando (left), named in tribute to the composer Lassus, was born here in 1583.[2]

Although he studied at Cambridge, Orlando Gibbons became such a respected figure that Oxford University awarded him an honorary doctorate before he was forty. This little almain is one of his simplest pieces; it could be played by waits in the streets for impromptu dancing by the riff-raff, or equally in the ballroom for ladies and gentlemen to step their more refined measures:

Gibbons's Almain

[1] cited in Hibbert, C (1987) *The English: A Social History* Guild
[2] Rowse, AL (1972) *The Elizabethan Renaissance* Macmillan

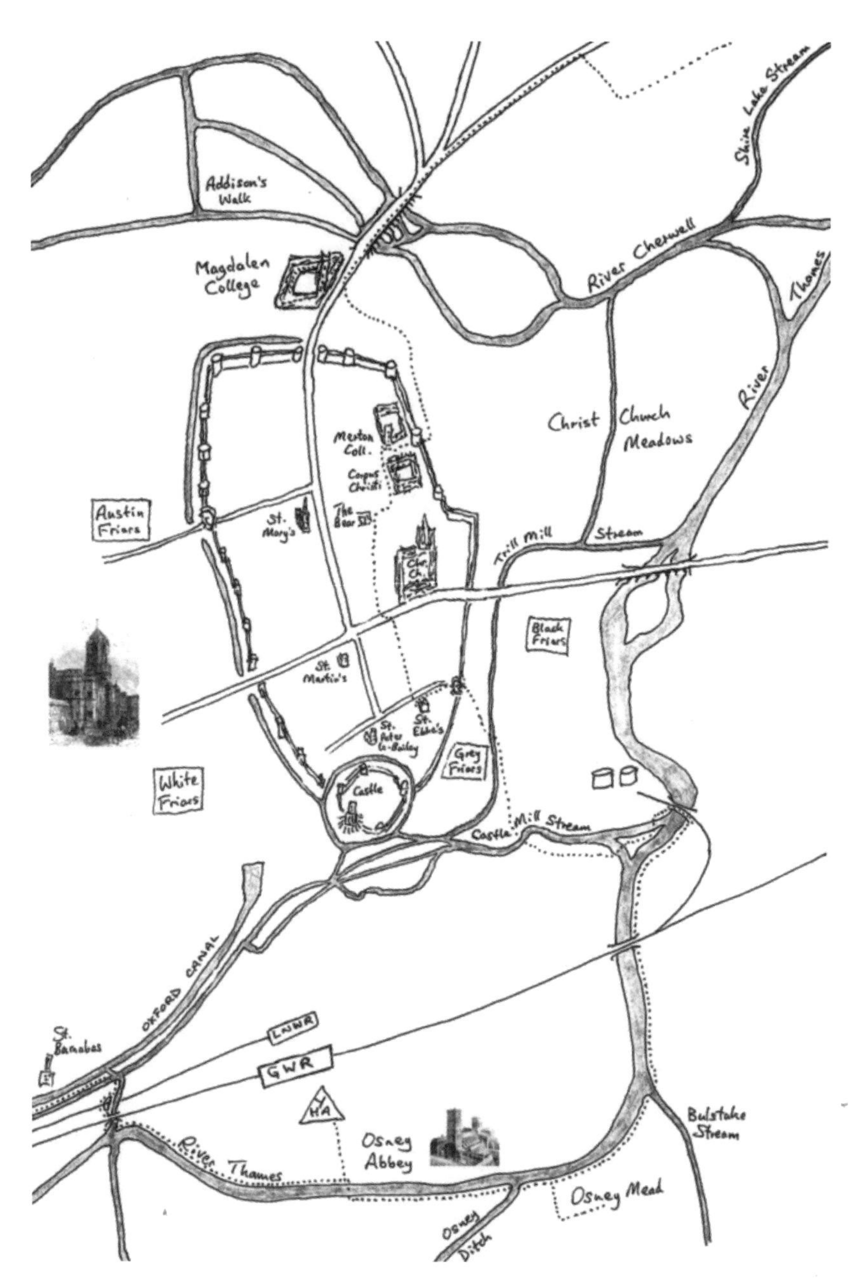

A selective map of central Oxford, showing features from different periods. Some ancient Oxford maps have south at the top; modern ones north at the top. For convenience this map has east at the top.

Two: Oxford to Sandford-on-Thames *(4 miles)*

The Flight – embarrassing misdemeanours – Addison's Walk – jewelweed – inscape – crow faithfulness – Wells Humour – humble access – inextinguishable candle – steel against steel – double save

25th October 2011

From the cosiness of the Bear, I headed out again into the back streets, past the butter-coloured stone of the old colleges with their memories of centuries of study and learning. The beautiful ornate façade of Oriel college conjured up a vague memory of an episode of *Morse* or perhaps its successor *Lewis* – which actually I prefer, the new character Hathaway being more interesting than his boss or his boss's predecessor. Increasingly the television series seems to focus on the colleges and their idiosyncratic world, in preference to urban scenes that could be part of any whodunnit.

Enjoying the architecture and atmosphere, I wandered down a broad path between Merton and Corpus Christi, listening to the curious chime of Merton's clock, that one writer finds 'reminiscent of a Gregorian plainchant'.[1]

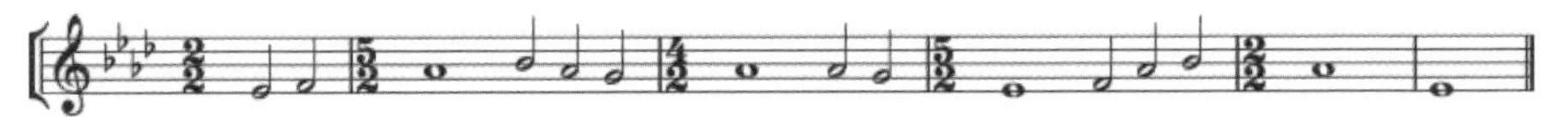

A tall iron gate gave access to Christ Church Meadow, but I didn't feel there was enough time to make a leisurely circuit of the whole of this huge green space. Instead I turned left along Dead Man's Walk, which ran along the outside of the old city wall. The corpse in question when the path was named would have been Jewish, for the name recalls that this was once the route from the Synagogue to the old Jewish burial ground outside the city walls. My eye was caught by a plaque commemorating the first English aeronaut, who took off from here in October 1784 in a fire balloon and landed four miles away in Woodeaton. The adrenaline must have been pumping for that man, floating free over the turrets and towers and domes, not knowing whether death by fire or by falling would interrupt his exhilarating flight.

The Flight

This tune dates from the same period, but could not have been written to commemorate the Oxford balloon flight, having been first published a few years before it took place; most probably it refers to a 'flight' in the sense of escape.

[1] Jubb, M (1980) *The Thames Valley Heritage Walk* Constable

Another tall gate marked the way back to the High Street, opposite the old tower of Magdalen, begun in 1492, which was the first tower in England to be adorned with a clock, in 1505. I tried to photograph it without getting in the way of the hordes of hurrying students passing over Magdalen Bridge. Students seem to change little with the passing centuries; an inspection at Magdalen College in the early sixteenth century uncovered the following embarrassing misdemeanours:

> Stokes was unchaste with the wife of a tailor.
> Stokysley baptized a cat and practised witchcraft.
> Gregory climbed the great gate by the tower, and brought a Stranger into College.
> Kendall wears a gown not sewn together in front.
> Pots and cups are very seldom washed, but are kept in such a dirty state that one sometimes shudders to drink out of them.
> Gunne has had cooked eggs at the Taberd in the middle of the night.
> Kyftyll played cards with the butler at Christmas time for money.
> Smyth keeps a ferret in College, Lenard a sparrow-hawk, Parkyns a weasel, while Morcott, Heycock and Smyth stole and killed a calf in the garden of one master Court.[1]

It would have been nice – but there wasn't time – to walk round Addison's Walk, the leafy waterside loop in the grounds of Magdalen, described by Celia Fiennes in 1694 as 'a very fine gravell walk, two or 3 may walk abreast, and rows of trees on either side, and this is round a water which makes it very pleasant.'[2] In the late 1920s Addison's Walk was the scene of a famous discussion between JRR Tolkien and CS Lewis, during which Tolkien finally convinced his as yet unbelieving friend that the Resurrection might be *both* an example of the widespread 'dying god' myth, symbol of winter giving way to spring, *and* a historical fact – the two were not necessarily mutually exclusive. So it was 'a myth that really happened', as Lewis phrased it when the penny finally dropped; and a little while later Lewis became a Christian.

Addison's was a favourite early morning walk of CS 'Jack' Lewis's for many years, and the story is told of his taking a guest with him one damp morning after overnight rain. They spotted an odd growth on a bush: '"That looks like my hat!" said Jack; then, joyfully, "It *is* my hat!" and clapping the sodden mass on to his head, he continued the walk.'[3]

[1] Hibbert, *op cit*
[2] Morris, C ed (1982) *The Illustrated Journeys of Celia Fiennes* Webb & Bower
[3] Lewis, WH ed (1966) *Letters of CS Lewis* Harcourt Brace

Joseph Addison did not create the walk, which had probably existed for a century or two before he enjoyed it during his time at Oxford, a little over three hundred years ago. He was sharply aware of the beauty of natural scenes, and liked the idea that it is not necessary to own land in order to enjoy it:

> A man of polite imagination is let into a great many pleasures, that the vulgar are not capable of receiving... He meets with secret refreshment in a description, and often feels a greater satisfaction in the prospect of fields and meadows, than another does in the possession. It gives him, indeed, a kind of property in everything he sees, and makes the most rude, uncultivated parts of nature administer to his pleasures...[1]

Thus writing a slow travel book can take the enjoyment of rambling through varied scenery, distil it, and offer it to many who are able to share that experience by virtue of their 'polite imagination'. I walked down the busy Iffley Road, past the University Sports Ground, scene of the first four-minute mile, before turning aside into the peace of Jackdaw Lane and Meadow Lane. The latter ran a long way behind houses; on the left an interesting mix of garden gates, fences, old sheds, garages, and newly-built properties fronting onto the lane; on the right a long grassy recreation space, the river beyond hidden by trees, as I thought, though in fact the Shire Lake Ditch ran behind the trees and the Thames was a little further off. The afternoon light was just beginning to dim slightly, until I turned right, crossing Donnington Bridge, a modern single span over the river, and found that the light on the crown of the bridge was considerably brighter, raised as it was above the flat surroundings.

Down on the far bank was the Thames Path, the continuous 213-mile route from Thames Head above Kemble to the Barrier at Woolwich, a mile or so of which I had already walked through Osney, as well as another mile near Eynsham, in Book 5. A single sculler came by, pulling easily upstream past an interesting variety of moored craft.

Beyond the moored boats several examples of a bright yellow flower caught the eye: Touch-me-not Balsam, also known as Jewel-weed, and here it did stand out like a jewel in the subdued light. The name might give the impression of a poisonous or stinging plant, but in fact it refers to the seed-pods, which explode when ripe, and which can go off suddenly if touched when they are almost ready. The plant is a food for the caterpillar of the Netted Carpet moth, which has cleverly developed the knack of nibbling through the fibres that would have triggered the seed-pod explosion, so that it can enjoy the green seeds at leisure.

[1] *The Spectator,* June 21, 1712

At Iffley Lock I was impressed by the ornate bridge over a short arm to a slipway. The channels and weir and lock gates and lock-keeper's house made a charming picture all together in the softly fading afternoon. It was not dark enough for things to be indistinct, but colours were perhaps just a little muted; and the overall effect was warm and comforting rather than gloomy, which gathering dusk can sometimes seem. Beyond the lock, the traffic hum of the Oxford By-Pass grew to a roar, until I passed under Isis Bridge and left it behind.

An arched footbridge then took the path over a wide side channel that looked like a closed backwater, since the willow trees leaned so far out over the water; in fact this was the combined flow of the Hinksey Stream, the Hogacre Ditch, and the Weirs Mill Stream, re-entering the main river and finally bringing together all the waters that had separated in such a profusion of channels and ditches and streams by or through Oxford. Some of that water had left the main channel of the Thames more than six miles before, at Hagley Pool, to flow past Wytham and Botley and Hinksey before rejoining here. Most of the side-channels would originally have been dug or deepened to power mills; medieval Oxford was full of mills. Some of the millstreams have since disappeared, but even today a straight line drawn through Carfax and projected due east and west crosses at least eight south-flowing streams.

Immediately ahead were the peeling grey tubular steel girders and arches of Kennington Railway Bridge, which had once carried the Great Western branch to Thame, and now survived only as an industrial siding to the BMW car plant in Cowley. Under the bridge, aerosol artists had sprayed a simple left-wing slogan: PEACE & SOCIALISM, which I mentally saluted in passing.

Beyond the bridge a stile gave access to an open meadow that ran right to the riverbank, so that the Thames Path no longer had the appearance of a towpath or riverside esplanade, but instead became a faintly traced path across the short grass that was being assiduously cropped by a sizeable mixed gaggle of Greylag and white domestic geese. The broad meadow gave a sense of expanded space and time, leading to a more relaxed stride past the geese, who happily showed no sign of aggression, stepping aside politely for the passing rambler.

I was conscious of walking where many famous feet had pressed the turf before; students and dons alike used to (and no doubt still do) escape from the ancient walls and towers into the green countryside. Tolkien and Lewis were great walkers, as was the poet Gerard Manley Hopkins in his undergraduate days; his journal mentions a walk this way, downriver to Sandford, carrying a book of Coventry Patmore's poems, but not, surely, with his nose buried in it as he walked, simply ready, perhaps, to pause, sit under a tree, and take the book out of his pocket to combine the experiences of poetry and nature. Hopkins too was aware of following those he admired, and sharing their experience in a later era; his inspiration was Duns Scotus' time in Oxford:

> …this air I gather and release
> He lived on; these weeds and waters, these walls are what
> He haunted who of all men most sways my spirits to peace;

Scotus was of great importance to Hopkins because of the stress he placed on the individuality, the uniqueness, of both people and things, paying particular attention to precisely those characteristics that differentiate one individual tree, flower, view, skyscape, personality or experience from another of the same type. Scotus coined the Latin word *haecceitas*, which translates as 'thisness', to describe this individuality; Hopkins preferred his own English coinage of 'inscape', a typically condensed word for the 'landscape of innermost being', which he saw as an expression of the infinitely varied creativity of God, who could not possibly create the same thing twice. Once this concept was clear in his mind, he saw inscape everywhere, and was continually grateful to Duns Scotus for helping to crystallise the idea, writing in his journal: 'when I took in any inscape of the sky or sea I thought of Scotus'.[1] He particularly saw how each of the temporary stages in a process of change was beautiful in itself: the gradual opening or withering of a flower, the constantly shifting patterns of cloud in the sky, or the successive colours in a slow sunset.

Poetry was not Hopkins' only talent; he was a fine artist, and used his eye for intricate detail and balanced composition to good effect in his poems. On top of that he had a sharp critical ear for music, loving particularly English composers and English folk melodies: '..in this we excel,' he wrote to a friend, 'and for tune, both stately and sweet … I never heard any national airs equal to the English'.[2] Purcell was a great favourite of his, and when he returned to Oxford briefly in 1879 he wrote a sonnet in homage to Purcell, praising his individuality:

> Not mood in him nor meaning, proud fire or sacred fear,
> Or love, or pity, or all that sweet notes not his might nursle:
> It is the forged feature finds me; it is the rehearsal
> Of own, of abrupt self there so thrusts on, so throngs the ear.[3]

A hornpipe from a late edition of Playford's English Dancing Master, a melody originally written by Purcell as incidental music for Congreve's play 'The Old Bachelor', gives some idea of what might have been running through Hopkins' head, as he tried to use words to express the beauty of music.

[1] House, H ed (1959) *Journals & Papers of Gerard Manley Hopkins* OUP
[2] Abbott, CC ed (2ed 1956) *Further Letters of Gerard Manley Hopkins* OUP
[3] Gardner, WH (1953) *Gerard Manley Hopkins* Penguin

Wells Humour

This reach of the Thames, near Kennington, had been the scene of sheep-roasts on the ice, in the hard winters of 1838, 1855, and 1871[1]; it was hard to imagine such cold now, on a balmy autumn afternoon. Opposite Rose Island was moored a narrowboat with a musical name: *Meet On The Ledge* of Cropredy. The associations with that most seminal of English folk-rock groups, Fairport Convention, were obvious: 'Meet on the Ledge' was an emotionally charged song with links to a traumatic motorway crash and the death of an early band member; Cropredy was where they sponsored an annual festival at which they played, sometimes together with former band members. A lean and weatherbeaten figure was setting off from the boat, struggling to get his bicycle upright and moving, while carrying a long and heavy plank which was making balance difficult. I wondered if he was just a fan, or a roadie or former band member; there had been so many.

Here the river widened and split, making a double bend in the process. On the far side of the river, in a likely spot where the water was still and shadowed, a shabby old dinghy lay motionless, occupied by two motionless shabby old men with fishing rods. Fishing usually appears to be an almost exclusively male occupation, and this picture of tranquillity might well have represented a temporary masculine retreat from feminine domestic bustle and upheaval.

On the near bank two crows perched on a fence; they might have been watching the scene on the river, or they might simply have been enjoying the late afternoon air, and the softness of the fading daylight. Not being able to tell hen crows from cocks, I wondered whether this pair of crows was perhaps also two old codgers escaping from their wives for a few relaxing hours on the riverbank.

Dear Mr Four Points Rambler,

My cousin Phoebe has told me all about you and your prejudice against crows. You could not be further from the mark than to suggest that our devoted husbands might desire to be quit of our company, even temporarily. They only leave us for a short while should they wish to locate some particularly tasty morsel as a love gift.

It is astonishing to all crows how sadly faint and evanescent is the love of humans for their chosen mates.

Yours truly, *Constance Crowe*

[1] Taunt, H (1875) *Illustrated Map of the Thames*

It was a well-deserved rebuke. Many species of birds remain loyal to their mates by nature and instinct; they make no promises, neither do they need to worry about their partners straying. Other species are openly promiscuous, polygamous, or polyandrous; monogamy is not attempted. Only humans aspire to constancy and fail to achieve it.

Wondering at how everyone values faithfulness, even though few maintain it and some barely attempt it, I wandered on down-river to Fiddler's Elbow, where I crossed the footbridge over the channel leading to Sandford Pool. There was still light enough to see Sandford Lock in the distance, though a darkening of the sky beyond it hinted at an approaching shower. In fact as I came to the lock, with its cluster of white buildings, the first drops were falling, and I wondered whether to take shelter and swift refreshment in the King's Arms, a pub with some history.

The honourable John Byng was here in 1792, on a boat trip downriver from Oxford. He thought it 'a neat public house … and our bread and cheese, and cyder was handed to us by a gay drest-out lass; an additional incitement to parties of pleasure?'[1] I hesitated, but there was not long to go before the bus back to Oxford was due, and an information board showed clearly that I had another half-mile to walk up the lane to the main road where the bus would pass.

As the rain was still only spitting, it seemed best to head rapidly across the various footbridges to the far bank of the river, and up the lane to the church, all the while hoping that the rain would hold off and that there would be a shelter at the bus stop, and that I would get there before the bus. Hopes were more or less fulfilled, for just in the last hundred yards, the rain suddenly intensified to a real downpour, inspiring a quick trot to the shelter, at which the bus immediately appeared, allowing me to steam off inside as it swept in towards the darkening city.

I got off in the High, near what had once been a record shop; I remembered my delight at finding a box set of Schubert: the complete piano sonatas from Deutsche Grammophon, best quality in the days of vinyl, but marked down in a sale to a price I could afford. That shop, once a source of wonderful music, was now a restaurant. I went through the covered market in search of anything of interest, but it was almost completely closed for the day, and so I moved on to Blackwell's bookshop. This proved much bigger than I remembered it, opening out like the Tardis from a modest shop front to a huge space like a public library, from where it took me some time to find a convoluted route up to the second-hand section.

[1] Andrews, CB ed (1934) *The Torrington Diaries* Eyre & Spottiswoode

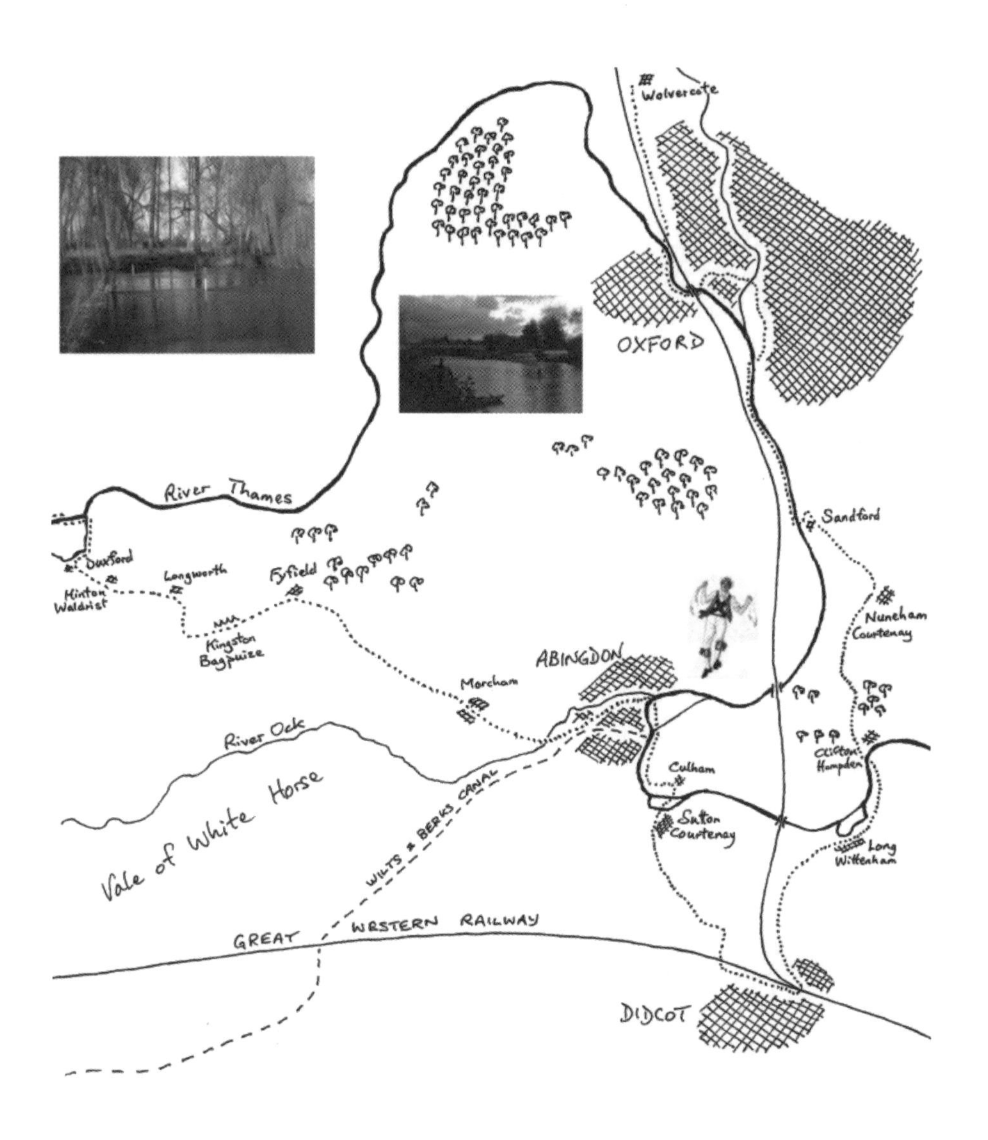

Map for chapters 1-6

(NB - as in all the maps in this book, the fine dotted line indicates the route taken.)

Blackwell's has long been such a universally respected institution that some have been tempted to a counter-reaction. The Inkling Hugo Dyson was not one to be daunted by a reputation, and his approach became a legend:

> Walking up to the counter he said: "I want a second hand so-and-so's Shakespeare; have you got one?" The assistant: "Not a second hand one sir, I'm afraid." Dyson (impatiently): "Well, take a copy and rub it on the floor, and sell it to me as shop soiled, it's all the same to me!"[1]

With a certain amount of hesitation and struggle against temptation, I managed to leave Blackwell's without buying anything, emerging into the brightly-lit bustle of the Broad, night by now having fully arrived. I headed west, past where the Oxford martyrs had been burnt alive for their resistance to the Marian counter-reformation in the 1550s. One of those martyrs was Thomas Cranmer, the author of my favourite prayer, indeed the only one I consistently missed when attending churches that did not use set prayers: the Prayer of Humble Access. Based as it is on various Bible verses, it has a timeless quality, as if it were one of the oldest parts of the liturgy, but it was freshly composed by the Archbishop of Canterbury in the days of Edward VI. The following is the 1552 version, the latest that Cranmer could have approved; but only tiny changes have been made since then.

> We do not presume to come to this thy Table, O merciful Lord, trusting in our own righteousness, but in thy manifold and great mercies. We be not worthy so much as to gather up the crumbs under thy Table. But thou art the same Lord, whose property is always to have mercy: Grant us therefore, gracious Lord, so to eat the flesh of thy dear Son Jesus Christ, and to drink his blood, that our sinful bodies may be made clean by his body, and our souls washed through his most precious blood, and that we may evermore dwell in him, and he in us.

The flowing rhythm of the words is at once a tonic and a balm. The hand that wrote that prayer was the hand that Cranmer held in the flame so that it would be burnt first, for it was the hand that had signed the recantations he was now ashamed of. At the last moment, as he was due to make a final spoken recantation, he dug in his heels and repudiated all that he had signed after a long imprisonment in the Bocardo jail, within sight of this memorial.

In contrast to the cautious Cranmer, Hugh Latimer's courage never wavered; he was no more cowed by Queen Mary than he had been by her father. In 1530 he challenged King Henry, speaking up for the common people:

> You have promised us the Word of God; perform your promise now rather than tomorrow! God will have the faith defended, not by man or man's power, but by His Word only, by the which He hath evermore defended it ... The day is at hand when you shall give an account of your office, and of the blood that hath been shed with your sword.[2]

[1] from Major W Lewis's diary, cited in Carpenter, H (1978). *The Inklings* Allen & Unwin
[2] d'Aubigné, JHM (1853) *The Reformation in England*

Not many dared speak like that to Henry VIII. It would be wonderful to count a man like Latimer among one's ancestors; unfortunately, it seems quite likely that I am descended from John Holyman, who was among those who tried and condemned him. On the point of death, Latimer (right) was still concerned to encourage others, urging his fellow-martyr: 'Be of good comfort, Master Ridley, and play the man! We shall this day light such a candle, by God's grace, in England, as I trust shall never be put out.'[1]

The candle was indeed never put out. Though many opposed the Gospel in later years, as in Latimer and Ridley's day, yet individuals kept calling for true repentance and submission. Two hundred years after the burning of martyrs outside the walls, William Romaine was in St Mary's church, preaching a sermon that gave considerable offence to some of the supposedly great and good of Oxford. In the morning of March 20, 1757, he took Isaiah 54:17 as his text, 'Their righteousness is of me, saith the Lord', and expounded it to show that none should consider themselves as *deserving* of salvation:

> This is the righteousness of God to which every sinner must submit, if he be ever discharged from condemnation. He must receive it from God as his free gift, without the least merit or deserving. And he must trust wholly to it, never presuming to add anything of his own to it as a condition of justification. These are hard lessons to the pride of our corrupt hearts. Indeed it is the hardest of grace to humble us so far, that we can give up the merit of all our fancied good works, and take righteousness as a free gift. As if God's righteousness was not perfect enough, we are always thinking to add something of our own to it.

The University Vice-chancellor, Dr Randolph of Corpus Christi, must have been a man who considered that his own uprightness and respectability, to say nothing of his exalted academic status, would automatically earn him a reserved seat at the top table in Heaven, for Romaine's sermon made him so angry that he saw to it that this impertinent preacher would never stand in a University-controlled pulpit again.[2] Perhaps he suspected that words such as the following were deliberately aimed at himself (and perhaps indeed they were, but not necessarily by the preacher):

> That man never saw the corruption and plague of his own heart, who dreams of working out for himself a righteousness, in which he may appear faultless at the bar of justice. Sin and pride have so blinded his eyes, that he knows not himself. He sees not how corrupt his nature nor how corrupt his life is, nor yet how corrupt his very best duties are.

[1] Foxe, J (1563) *Actes and Monuments of these Latter and Perillous Days*
[2] Ryle, JC (1885) *Christian Leaders of the 18th Century*

Before any ban could be decreed or take effect, Romaine preached his sermon again in the afternoon at St. Peter-le-Bailey, more or less on the spot where the Reformation in Oxford had begun in the last years of the 15th century. To St Mary's Hall, a college of Augustinian Canons, came Erasmus (opposite) to meet, discuss with, and learn from John Colet, who had begun lecturing on Romans. Colet (left) had lost patience with the so-called 'Schoolmen', who took the undeniable fact that a text may have more than one meaning, and exaggerated it to ridiculous extremes. They interpreted every sentence of Scripture not only literally, but also, and at greater length, tropologically, allegorically, and anagogically, building such a mountain of interpretation on each phrase or verse that it stood alone, with little reference to the verses around it.

Colet returned to the simple question: what does this text actually *say* – bearing in mind its context, its author and its intended readers? To the academics this seemed so straightforward as to be disrespectful of the mysteries of God's Word; but for those who had been flummoxed by the prevailing teaching, who perhaps wanted to apply the teaching of the Bible to their own lives, who had serious personal questions they wanted answers to, Colet's approach was a revelation, and his lectures were soon very well attended.

As an example of how helpful his teaching could be, consider how Colet resolves the issue of free will versus predestination, emphasising that, yes, God is sovereign, and all things happen according to His will, but He is no puppeteer, and we are not robots; we do have free will, but God is able to incorporate that into His plan:

> Thus you see that things are brought about by a providing and directing God, …not from any force from without (*illata*) — since nothing is more remote from force than the Divine action — but by the natural desire and will of man, the Divine will and providence secretly and silently, and, as it were, naturally accompanying (*comitante*) it, and going along with it so wonderfully, that whatever you do and choose was known by God, and what God knew and decreed to be, of necessity comes to pass.[1]

Erasmus, although already leaning in this direction, and much attracted to Colet's thought, nevertheless took time to accept it completely, and the friends (both were just over 30 years old) had many an argument, both face to face and later by letter. However their disagreements were productive, for neither wished to win an argument simply for the sake of their own pride, and both were passionately concerned to reach true understanding. As Colet wrote to Erasmus:

[1] Seebohm, F (1867) *The Oxford Reformers*

> In the meantime do you patiently hear me, and let us both, if, when striking our flints together, any spark should fly out, eagerly catch at it. For we seek, not for victory in argument, but for *truth*, which perchance may be elicited by the clash of argument with argument, as sparks are by the clashing of steel against steel!

New Inn Hall Street, where Colet lived, used to be called Seven Deadly Sins Lane, though nobody seems to know why. Gerard Manley Hopkins lodged there in 1866, and was living there when he left the Anglican Church and was received as a Catholic; God called him in the opposite direction to many others. He would surely have known the old name of the address of his lodgings, and been amused, though he might have been less amused if he had known that after his time there, the street would gradually become a focus for Low Church and non-conformist evangelicalism. St Peter's College was founded in the 20th century, to provide low-cost accommodation for less well-off students, and always had an evangelical bias. I had a friend there, and while I was working at Kemp Hall Bindery, I often found it convenient to join Paul for Saturday lunch, since I worked till twelve on a Saturday.

It was a friendly place, very down to earth and non-snooty, and on the day of the FA cup final I took the chance to slip into the TV room to see Sunderland take on Leeds United, who were then at the peak of their achievement, dominating the old First Division, while Sunderland were mid-table in the Second, and were not expected to put up much resistance. Nevertheless two Makem lads had bagged the sofa in the front row, and were well stocked with beer and optimism; and as the match unfolded their optimism rose till it was off the scale. First, the left-footed Porterfield, on a rare foray into the penalty area, scored with a right-footed volley; then Montgomery managed the famous double save, denying Lorimer, the hardest shot in the game, at close range. By the end of the game the two Wearside students were on their feet, hugging each other, swaying ecstatically amid the debris of red-and-white scarves and empty beercans, murmuring 'We're going to get drunk tonight! We're going to get *drunk* tonight!'

Three: Sandford-on-Thames to Didcot *(8 miles)*

Dropping sweetness – out of bounds – Christ Church Bells – Bible translation – burning the tares – clumping earth – the Kite Hornpipe – picturesque travel – stranded Mayor – model museum – Great Western preservation

26th October 2011

The following morning, looking in the High Street for the next bus to Sandford, I found there was a considerable wait, so I crossed the road to head for Christ Church Meadow. Once again I passed the Bear Inn and Oriel College, and peered into Corpus Christi College, which today was closed to visitors, so that I could only see a vision through a gateway of that pleasant quadrangle, around which, according to the founder, 'scholars, like ingenious bees are by day and night to make wax to the honour of God, and honey, dropping sweetness, to the profit of themselves and of all Christians'.[1] I could almost smell the honey.

As I was about to turn down the alleyway by Merton chapel, I heard organ music, and went for a closer look and listen. The door stood open, and I slipped inside. The space was wide and empty of chairs or pews; sunlight streamed in from one corner; to one side was a wooden screen beyond which was an older-looking, darker transept. High on the other side in an ornate gallery sat a girl organist with flowing waist-length hair, playing Bach.

A young man came in from the street, carrying some PA equipment. I was about to ask him if photography was permitted, but he spoke first, hurriedly.

'Sorry,' he said, 'did you just come in through that door?' His manner was open, not hostile, and slightly embarrassed. 'You're not allowed in here, I'm sorry.' Perhaps he should not have left the door open, and was feeling guilty. I apologised and left, carrying with me jumbled impressions of privilege transgressed, of sunlit stone, of the short wide pages of the music book at the organ, of the inexorably steady pulse of the music. I later found that what I had at a glance taken to be a transept was actually the main nave of Merton College chapel, and I had just been in the west end, almost like a large foyer, an open space for the sound of the organ to fill and overflow.

Outside at this relatively early hour (at least for tourists and students, if not for workers) it was still cool and quiet. I went through the gate into Christ Church Meadow, and found another gate to my right that gave a view of the east end of Christ Church chapel, or Oxford Cathedral, the only cathedral that doubles as a college chapel.

Christ Church bells are commemorated in a lively Restoration catch, written in 1673 by Henry Aldrich, Dean of the cathedral and man of many parts: classical scholar, theologian, architect, heraldist, and composer. Dean Aldrich was responsible for much of the architecture of Christ Church college as it is today; he was not shy of making sure that his talents were fully employed and recognised in his ecclesiastical capacity, as well as in his leisure time, as in the little composition opposite.

[1] Bishop Foxe, cited in Morris, J (1978) *The Oxford Book of Oxford* OUP

Restoration catches were usually very bawdy, though not always in their original text; sometimes the rudeness only appeared when they were sung in parts, as they were designed to be. The following goes in three-part canon, and is said to be the only surviving catch to be singable in respectable company. Its happy lightheartedness captures the relief of Restoration society that the years of civil war and Commonwealth were over, as well as hinting at the shallowness of the new era.

Hark! The bonny Christ Church bells, one, two, three, four, five, six
They sound so woundy great, so wondrous sweet
And they troll so merrily, merrily.

Hark! The first and second bell that every day at four and ten
Cries come, come, come, come, come to prayers
And the verger troops before the Dean.

Tingle tingle ting goes the small bell at nine to call the bearers home
But de'il a man will leave his can
Till he hears the mighty Tom.

The dean (right) was apparently a pipe-smoker, and it is said that the catch gives space for a pull on the pipe to keep it alight while singing.[1] The key given here is chosen to be comfortable for most singers, as well as giving a good resonant last low note to represent the boom of Great Tom.

The Mighty Tom was 'Thomas of Osney', the clock bell from the dissolved Osney Abbey, seven feet in diameter, seven tons in weight; named originally for St Thomas of Canterbury, he was renamed 'Mary' when transferred to Christ Church during the reign of Mary I, but soon resumed his ancient name. He is said to have been inscribed: 'IN THOMAE LAUDE RESONO BIM BOM SINE FRAUDE'; that is, 'in praise of Thomas I ring out ding dong without deceit'.

[1] Betjeman, J (1938) *An Oxford University Chest* John Miles

The point of the porters refusing to finish their drinks until they heard Great Tom's deep note was that he was rung at five past nine, traditionally tolling 101 times; so the little bell at nine gave them convenient warning of drinking-up time.

A generation before the urbane polymath Dean Aldrich ran Christ Church, a very different man, the Puritan John Owen, had been Dean here, keen to shake all those listening to his sermons into a sense of their own sinfulness. He was uncompromisingly blunt about human inadequacy and depravity: 'the man that understands the evil of his own heart, how vile it is, is the only useful, fruitful, and solidly believing and obedient person,' as well as the particular hindrance of pride: 'the Word of God is a troublesome inmate to an unhumbled mind and heart.'

Yet he could also be gentle and positive, and reassuring to the genuinely repentant that forgiveness is always possible, due to the infinite love and concern of Christ for the lost sheep:

> Jesus Christ yet stands before sinners, calling, inviting, encouraging them to come unto him… 'Why will ye not have compassion on your own souls? … lay aside all procrastinations, all delays; put me off no more; …do not so hate me as that you will rather perish than accept of deliverance from me.[1]

Compassion was not always something that the church authorities practised; they were often keener to maintain the status quo. More than a century before Owen was preaching and writing in Christ Church, in 1528, when it was still Cardinal College, the agents of Cardinal Wolsey were rounding up students found to have been distributing Tyndale's newly translated English New Testament, secretly imported from Holland. Those caught were not gently handled.

> Under Cardinal College there was a deep cellar sunk in the earth, in which the butler kept his salt fish. Into this hole these young men, the choice of England, were thrust. The dampness of this cave, the corrupted air they breathed, the horrible smell given out by the fish, seriously affected the prisoners, already weakened by study. Their hearts were bursting with groans, their faith was shaken, and the most mournful scenes followed one another in this foul dungeon. The wretched captives gazed on one another, wept, and prayed.[2]

The students were later brought out of the cellar, marched in forced penitence to burn their books at Carfax, and then most of them were returned to their salt fish dungeon, whence some never emerged alive. It is shocking to us today to think how adamantly Church and State believed that it was dangerous for citizens to think for themselves, and to read God's Word in their own mother tongue.

[1] Owen, J (1684) *The Glory of Christ*
[2] d'Aubigné, *op cit*

But men with egos as great as Wolsey's, the butcher's son who had risen by his own considerable effort and wit to wear the chain of the Chancellorship of the land, to say nothing of the hat of a cardinal, could not tolerate the blow to their pride if every man in the land should understand the Bible. There would be no mistaking plain words such as Tyndale's rendering of Ephesians 2, verses 8 and 9: 'For by grace are ye made safe thorowe fayth and that not of youre selves. For it is the gyfte of God and commeth not of workes lest eny man shuld bost him silfe.' For more than a century the danger to the rich and powerful, should Holy Scripture be available in everyday language, had been apparent; Wycliffe's translation of those same verses was even pithier: 'For bi grace ye ben sauyd bi feith, and this not of you; for it is the yifte of God, not of werkis, that no man haue glorie.'

IOHANNES WICLEFUS, Theol. Angl

In Wycliffe's day, the late 14th century, the freethinking in the university was more widespread, and harder for the church to suppress. Here in this same place, before it became a college, when it was still St Frideswide's Priory, one of Wycliffe's associates was able to preach in his support, with the university authorities' blessing:

> ...the preacher boldly defended the orthodoxy of Wyclif's doctrine of the Eucharist... As the chancellor [Robert Rygge] retired in state from St Frideswide's, followed by the whole concourse of doctors and masters, he made a point of waiting for the preacher at the church door, and walked home with him 'laughing and great joy came upon the Lollards at such a sermon'.[1]

The Lollards' joy was at the prospect that a corrupt church would be renewed; over the centuries the organised church had wandered far from its true calling, and much that was against all Biblical teaching was done in the church's name.

Hundreds of years earlier still, on St Brice's Day, 13th November 1002, St Frideswide's Priory had not been the scene of laughter and joy, but of screams and despair, the roar of blazing timbers and the stench of burning flesh. Fleeing from a xenophobic pogrom authorised by King Æthelræd II, the Danes of Oxford broke into the priory church and barricaded themselves inside. Inevitably the English then burned down church and refugees together. The king's charter, issued in 1004 for the rebuilt priory, is a nauseating piece of self-justification, representing the massacre as 'most just', and the burning of the church as 'compelled by necessity'.

He had been advised, he wrote, to eliminate the Danish settlers, 'who had sprung up in this island, sprouting like cockle amongst the wheat'. While Danish longships were harrying the coasts, and Danish war-hosts were raiding inland on a regular basis in the years leading up to the millennium, numerous individual Danes had been settling peacefully and becoming part of English society. Unfortunately a few of these settlers had joined the raiding armies.

[1] Rashdall, H (1895) *Universities of Europe in the Middle Ages*

Possibly they had had their arms twisted to do so, but still it was not surprising that this made the king and his advisors very nervous about the potential for treachery.

The phrase 'cockle amongst the wheat' is a striking echo of the parable in Matthew 13 about the wheat and tares – although not an exact copy of the Vulgate Latin, which has 'zinzania in medio tritici', while Æthelræd's charter says 'lolium inter triticum'. Zinzania, also the word in the original Greek New Testament, is wild rice; but lolium, particularly lolium temulentum, is probably the plant that Jesus actually intended His listeners to imagine. Known in English as darnel or cockle, it looks very like wheat at every stage until it is fully ripe, when the difference finally becomes clear (left). At the end of the parable (the harvest) the darnel is to be gathered first and burnt.

It is not impossible that some zealous nationalist among the English churchmen had argued that it was time to do the gathering and burning. Many thought that the year 1000 heralded the end of the age (thus time for the harvest), and the English were nominally Christian while many of the Danes were still, in theory and often in practice, pagan. It therefore required no great feat of imagination to see the English as the wheat and the Danes as the tares or cockle. Ironically, those so-called Christians among the English who were nurturing hatred and murder in their hearts were the true examples of tares among the wheat (cf 1John 1:9).

I would have liked to have a quick look inside the college, or at least inside the cathedral, scene of so great and varied a history. It was open to visitors, but the charge, even with a seniors' discount, was far too high for a brief visit to be worthwhile. I turned away and walked along the broad avenue, between Merton Fields on my left and Christ Church Meadow stretching away on the right. Grey squirrels scampered across the gravel, but few pedestrians were about.

Christ Church Meadow is so beautiful, and so important to both town and university as a green space, that it is disturbing to think that there were serious proposals, in the mid-20th century, for a major road to be routed through it as a way of easing Oxford's traffic problems. Fortunately the number of Christ Church graduates in very high places (including the cabinet) at that time meant that the scheme was firmly quashed.

I strolled over Magdalen Bridge again and found a convenient bus stop on the Iffley Road, where I passed the time waiting for the bus in observing the varied attire, approach, and speed of the cyclists on their way into town: smart, scruffy, stylish or studious, cautious, confident or cavalier; and so numerous that the motorised traffic had to give them priority. The bus, when it finally arrived, whisked its passengers rapidly through the southern suburbs of Oxford, the part of the town that Betjeman called 'Motopolis', and of which he complained that it was 'indistinguishable from Swindon, Neasden, or Tooting Bec'.[1]

[1] Betjeman, *op cit*

It is a common complaint today; we think of it as a 21st century problem, and it is a surprise to find Betjeman already writing 'chain-stores have taken the place of small shop-keepers' in 1938.

Leaving the bus at Sandford, I walked a couple of hundred yards back down the lane, past the neat little Norman church, where the Rev Charles Dodgson, the author of *Alice in Wonderland*, had preached his first sermon.

I wanted to find the green lane towards Nuneham, and so be sure that I was picking up the route where I had left it. The access to the track was difficult to distinguish from domestic driveways, leading to some anxiety about being on the right route, but it soon became a pleasant grassy path between low hedges, allowing views of meadows sloping away down to the river; the low sun ahead gleaming on the wet grass. It was good to be back on the Four Points Ramble route; there had been so much fascinating history in Oxford that the sense of an ongoing journey had been somewhat obscured.

A stile led into open fields and easy walking past Lower Farm, as far as the first change of direction. This meant crossing a ploughed field, but it was possible to ignore the direct line of the right of way, and hug the nearby edge of the field, where the hard going was dotted with thistles and burdock.

In the next field I made the mistake of going straight across, following tractor tracks between dark green brassica shoots. The earth appeared dry, but was just damp and clayey enough to clump under pressure; so instead of building up round the sides of the boots, as often happens in a really muddy field, it built up underneath. Within every few strides I would find myself walking on wobbly irregular four-inch platforms that had to be kicked off, only to build up again.

It was a relief to reach the far side of the field, and then onto the main road, where the hard tarmac, and coarse grass verge, gradually cleaned off the clay. The road itself was broad enough for reasonably safe walking, facing the northbound traffic, but the persistent roar and whoosh of passing vehicles soon became irritating, and I was glad to turn aside on a gravel track. In the neighbouring meadow a red kite was poking about on the ground, presumably seeking beetles or worms; at intervals it rose and soared, displaying its long wings and forked tail in the sunlight.

Unfortunately the track proved not to be the path to Nuneham Park, and I had to return for another two hundred yards of the main road, pausing occasionally to tip my head back and enjoy the view of the kite as it sailed overhead time and again, eventually to be harassed by a cheeky little black-headed gull. The kite cruised impassively onwards, ignoring its zigzagging persecutor.

I found the right path by the pub, leading away from the neat houses lining the road – a neatness that the Reverend William Gilpin, Prebendary of Salisbury, passing through on his way to Cumberland, found less than picturesque:

> The village of Nuneham, through which the road passes, was built by Lord Harcourt for his cottagers; and with that regularity, which perhaps gives the most convenience to the dwellings of men. For this we readily relinquish the picturesque idea. Indeed I question, whether it were possible for a single hand to build a picturesque village. Nothing contributes more to it, than the various styles in building, which result from the different ideas of different people. When all these little habitations happen to unite harmoniously; and to be connected with the proper appendages of a village – a winding road – a number of spreading trees – a rivulet with a bridge – and a spire, to bring the whole to an apex;– the village is compleat.[1]

Gilpin's late 18th-century travel books, with their constant search for the 'picturesque', were highly influential, changing the way many people looked at landscape. He was careful to admit that there were other kinds of beauty, but he chose to restrict himself to a description of objects or scenes 'which please from some quality, capable of being illustrated by painting.'[2]

I wondered whether the day's walk would provide a scene nearer Gilpin's ideal; Clifton Hampden seemed a likely candidate. The path soon joined a lane; nearby, a middle-aged man was using a chainsaw to reduce a fallen tree to logs of manageable size. The little grey tractor, waiting to have its trailer filled with logs, was probably older than its owner. We agreed that it was a lovely morning, which it certainly was: bright and clear, with a cool wind that was welcome if you were taking exercise.

The lane to Nuneham Park was long, and partly shadowed by tall trees, over which two or three buzzards floated. On telephone wires a kestrel sat until I came quite close, at which it swooped away to perch on a distant pole. So I had seen three different birds of prey in less than a mile's walking – of which the red kite was certainly the most impressive.

Kite Hornpipe

[1] Gilpin, W (1786) *Observations, relative chiefly to Picturesque Beauty*
[2] Gilpin, W (1794) *Three Essays on Picturesque Beauty*

The public right of way led past the gates of the stately home, now an interfaith Global Retreat Centre. Neat little signs directed walkers away from the entrance; but a view of the fine façade could be glimpsed through the grand gateway. Of course the classic view of Nuneham House was from the other side, the west, to include the Thames in the setting. I was glad to see what little I could; at any rate, more than poor Gilpin, who was 'the less able … to speak with any precision of the beauty of these scenes, as a wet evening prevented our examining them, as we could have wished.'

I was well able to look around in the autumn sunshine, cooled by a brisk south-south-easterly breeze, as the track continued southwards between broad fields, over a low hill and down to New Cottage, where the route to Clifton bent sharply left as far as Keeper's Cottage. This (probably very desirable) residence was discreetly screened by a tall hedge, through which could be glimpsed a picturesque thatched roof. Alongside Roundhill Wood the path bent south again, following the edge of the wood past Thame Lane. More red kites were wheeling overhead, and one stayed around long enough to make photographs possible, the sun picking out the lighter patches under its long wings.

Ahead, the path sloped straight down to Clifton Hampden, clustered amid much greenery by the river; further on, the cooling towers of Didcot Power Station marked the end of the day's walk, now appearing well within reach. An alleyway within the village led past very picturesque redbrick thatched cottages with homely mature gardens, 'varied habitations united harmoniously', as in Gilpin's ideal; and the Thames and its handsome Victorian brick bridge, over which the road wound with charming curves, made a variety of fine views from different angles – not least from the triangular pedestrian refuges on the bridge itself, looking back at the church, with its neat little spire rising above the different trees standing along the cliff above the river. Henry Taunt thought it 'very pretty, quaint old cottages peep out from amid the greenery, and the spirelet of the church overtops and makes a centre point…' He also reported that even the fish were drawn to the spot:

> 'I don't know if the barbel come to listen to the music in the church, or whether they are a religious fish', (says one of the fishermen), 'but they always get round the church, and more on Sunday than any other day in the week.'[1]

[1] Taunt, *op cit*

Until the bridge was built, this had been the site of a ferry and ford for hundreds of years; and it was only when the Lord Mayor of London was making a stately progress downriver, and his barge ran aground here, leaving him ignominiously stuck for hours until the river level could be raised temporarily, that new locks were constructed and river levels managed more carefully. These improvements to navigation did not stop the ferry operating, but cattle could no longer easily ford the river, so a bridge became essential, and it was eventually built by Henry Gibbs, the lord of the manor, who engaged the best architect he could find, George Gilbert Scott, and took him out to dinner. It is said that the initial sketch of the bridge was made on Scott's shirt-cuff at the dinner-table.

From the bridge to Long Wittenham was unavoidable roadwalking without a pavement, stepping aside onto a narrow verge at frequent intervals. I passed the famous Barley Mow Inn, subject of a classic picture postcard watercolour by AR Quinton. The inn was still thatched, but of course there were no longer horses tethered outside, and the scene looked quite different with the tarmac and white lines of a busy B road, instead of the beaten earth road of a hundred years before.

For the last few hundred yards there was a raised walkway, which made for easier and safer walking, though it would not have been so safe if walkers in opposite directions had met, for it was narrow, with a three-foot drop to the road on one side, and a bigger drop to a deep and muddy ditch on the other. I was glad to meet nobody before I reached the impossibly pretty village of Long Wittenham, with another selection of well-kept old redbrick cottages, whose variety would have pleased the Reverend Gilpin, though he might well have objected to the straightness of the long main street. The church too looked attractive, tucked away modestly behind timbered houses, and I would have investigated if only I had had unlimited time available.

The village is fifteen hundred years or more in age, with evidence of human occupation for many centuries even before that. My eye was caught by the ancient beams of a cottage that was nevertheless very smartly and soundly maintained: Cruck Cottage may be as much as eight hundred years old, and thus one of the oldest dwellings in the area, but is clearly well loved and looked after.

There were a couple of benches in the centre of the village, giving a welcome opportunity for a short rest and a drink of water. The map marked a museum in the village, and I had seen signposts to 'Pendon Museum', which rang a faint bell in my memory: of a classic finescale model railway layout I had long ago read an article about. I wondered if this might be the same; complete serendipity if so, for I had not noticed it when planning the route through Long Wittenham.

The museum was a few hundred yards further on, and to my delight it *was* the model layout. I cannot quite explain why I am attracted to models; it is not just railways, but miniaturisation of any kind. In this case there were Dartmoor tors, thatched cottages, bullnose Morris cars, fields and farmyards, all with great attention to detail. But naturally the classic Great Western locomotives and rolling stock were a major feature, and it was nice to see them in 1:76 scale shortly before seeing the real thing later on.

The story behind the museum was a heart-warming one of how the vision of an 18-year-old Australian gradually became reality over several decades. In the late 1920s Roye England was already a modeller, already in love with the grace and elegance of the shining GW engines, and the lush green farming country they ran through, when he became aware that the old thatched houses were beginning to disappear, and modernisation was affecting the countryside.

He decided to model specific buildings to preserve their detailed appearance within an authentic landscape, including the trains, the make-up of which he recorded with academic thoroughness, every single carriage and van, in order that all details should be historically accurate. Nevertheless, the original focus was on village architecture rather than trains, although the trains may well attract the bulk of the visitors today.

The project proceeded slowly, as model-making projects do, but gradually picked up collaborators and eventually found a home in a youth hostel, before its present purpose-built shed was constructed in 1971, forty years after the first model inside had been started. By the time Roye England died in 1995, the Pendon Museum was well established.

I could have stayed there for hours, but decided to press on to the Didcot Railway Centre in time for a very late lunch. The path to Didcot, running alongside the Moor Ditch, turned out to be a level metalled cycleway, a section of Sustrans' National Route 5, some of which I had already walked north of Woodstock (see Book 5). There were extensive views across the fields; the spire of Appleford Church in the middle distance almost made a picture, but there were wires in the way.

A broad meadow contained so many gulls that collectively they made a wide white stripe across the green turf: mostly Black-headed, but also many Lesser Black-backed gulls. On the path itself was a little spot of vivid iridescent greeny-turquoise: a Rose Chafer beetle, *cetonia aurata*. Another flash of colour proved to be a Red Admiral butterfly; but generally the scene was in subdued early autumn colours: old greens, some yellow in the trees, the brown of burdock and teazle alongside the path, the grey towers of the power station looming ever closer.

The roar of traffic on a busy main road ahead made me apprehensive of a dangerous crossing; but in fact the cycleway ran in a tunnel under the embankment, the Moor Ditch flowing alongside. I was fortunate to be passing through in a spell of generally dry weather, for the tunnel was apparently liable to flooding, causing numerous complaints. Now the stream was flowing comfortably, neither full nor low, with very clear water containing a lot of fish.

Beyond the tunnel the cycleway became suburban, with lampposts, benches and modern landscaping: the Ladygrove Loop, as signs proclaimed. The sound of a chuffing steam engine floated on the breeze, and white smoke appeared behind the young trees that fringed the footpath. Footsore (indeed blistered) and hungry as I was, it was good to feel that journey's end was very near. Yet the Ladygrove Loop, curving steadily eastwards, seemed to go on for miles without ever coming to Didcot station; and in the sky ahead were unmistakable signs of an approaching heavy shower.

I continued to hope that I could reach the Great Western Society's centre before the rain began. Passing a playground, I saw that the boys on their BMX bikes were still happily swooping around the concrete curves; parents were still unconcernedly pushing prams; perhaps I was being unduly pessimistic, but the black cloud was now almost overhead. And then as the first drops fell, the BMX bikers overtook me in a panic-pedalling posse, disappearing to their nearby homes on the estate. There was no entrance to the centre from this side of the railway, as I had hoped, and by the time I had walked round to the far side and paid my way into the Didcot Railway Centre, I was quite damp. But the various shuttle services around the yard and sidings that make up the Didcot Railway Centre provided opportunities to dry off a little, as well as avoiding the rest of the heavy shower, and the refreshment room still had a few portions of lunch left at nearly three o'clock.

Unlike other preservation societies, where often the restoration of a line was the main focus, here there was more of a museum and exhibition atmosphere, and it was possible to dodge further showers in well-laid-out sheds full of GWR history and memorabilia. The original locomotive depot, with numerous ancillary sheds, had been well preserved and adapted, without any modern architecture to disturb the atmosphere of the age of the steam railway.

Like the Pendon Museum, the Great Western Society was originally the product of teenage enthusiasm, in this case even younger and bolder. In April 1961, four friends in their mid-teens, deep in discussion as they spotted trains from the Southall footbridge, grumbled that certain much-loved types of GWR locomotive were not scheduled to be officially preserved; so they decided to set up their own fund, and wrote to the Railway Magazine:

> SIR, - I am thinking of launching a campaign to purchase a "14XX" (former "48XX") class 0-4-2 tank locomotive from British Railways, with the purpose of preserving it in running order. The cost is £1,130, plus extras such as having "48XX" number-plates cast and repainting in Great Western livery. If sufficient support is obtained, perhaps a pull-and-push coach also might be preserved. I appeal to all those who could support this suggestion to get in touch with me at 14, Heldman Close, Hounslow, Middlesex.
>
> J.L. BARLOW

Youthful optimism and tenacity prevailed, and the initiative launched at the cost of a threepenny stamp (old money) has become a complex operation with stock to a value of many millions. In the startlingly bright sunny intervals between the drenching showers, I had the chance to look at several immaculately restored locomotives, copper and brass gleaming in the sunlight, everything from the industrious little pannier tank chuffing eagerly around, to magnificent express engines on static display. The only exhibit I avoided approaching was 6023 *King Edward II*, newly repainted in blue.

Admittedly it was 'authentic', in that British Railways did paint the Kings blue when experimenting with liveries soon after nationalisation, but a blue King is still an abomination that should in no way be encouraged. It looks as odd on rails as a blue king would on a wooden chessboard. This has little to do with only liking what one is used to, or being a stickler for authenticity; certain design styles suit certain colours, and squeal at other colours. An Ivatt 2-6-0 in Midland red is anachronistic and inauthentic, but still looks excellent; while a GWR 'Hall' in red looks weird, on the big screen or in real life. The standard GWR Churchward look: taper boiler, copper-capped chimney, brass safety-valve bonnet and all, only looks right with Middle Chrome Green paintwork and the number on the bufferbeam.

All too soon it was time to head for Didcot station and my modern train home; though as I waited I could paint a mental picture of 5039 *Rhuddlan Castle*, in the livery just described, with a string of chocolate-and-cream coaches, racing through at 95mph on the 'Cheltenham Flyer', as recorded in 1937.[1] This vision of the splendour of the Great Western contrasted with another Didcot image: two exhausted enginemen leaving the cab of their freight locomotive at three in the morning.

> We climbed down from her utterly worn out, for she had given us both a bad time. A 28XX would have waltzed that load up through the tunnel without any trouble, but we had to have No. 3030 'Dirty Gertie'.[2]

'Dirty Gertie' was one of the First-World-War-surplus ex-GCR 2-8-0s that the GWR bought at a bargain price from the Railway Operating Division. They were meant to be a stop-gap, just to run for a few years till they fell apart, but they were so ruggedly built that they lasted decades, despite total neglect, and the contempt of all GW men who found them sluggish and ugly: '…shambling, pitching, and thumping,' '…this great hulking brute…' were two typical descriptions.

[1] Nock, OS (1972) *GWR Steam* David & Charles

[2] Gasson, H (1976) *Footplate Days* Oxford Publishing Co

Four: Didcot to Abingdon *(6 miles)*

Waste Management – harvest wasted – crocodylus oxoniensis – defunct Lion – Butcher's Hornpipe – Springbok Stew – Goose and Gridiron – Swift Ditch – tutored prince – busy abbot – three bridges

11th January 2012

I returned to Didcot on a January day that was neither wet nor cold: cool and fresh rather than positively mild; ideal walking weather. Arriving at midday, having lunched early on the train, I shouldered a light rucksack and set off westwards alongside the railway. Even though the hours of daylight were limited, there was plenty of time for the short distance I planned to cover that day.

The map marked two paths northwards, either side of a sewage works and an industrial estate. I decided to take the first, as being further from the power station; this was almost certainly a mistake, though it would be some time before that became apparent. A lane led over the main line and the west-to-north spur; as I crossed, a London-bound express whooshed underneath at high speed, clearly not planning to stop at Didcot.

The bridleway was well signposted, down a lane shadowed by ivy-smothered trees. Somewhere high above the dark green leaves a robin sang. A man and a spaniel came towards me; as they passed, the dog made a sudden violent lunge in my direction, to be brought up short by his stout lead; probably just excitable friendliness.

The stench as I passed the sewage works came not from the sewage, but from a stagnant ditch on the other side of the lane, where the water was black with rotting vegetation. The industrial estate beyond was inoffensive, if not very picturesque; beyond that, the view widened, to include an extensive rubbish tip on the left, and broad fields on the right. Birds soared overhead: many gulls, a few crows, and largest of all, half a dozen red kites, some floating low enough for their russet colouring to be admired, as well as their long wings and elegantly forked tails.

The smells that came and went as the breeze shifted could have been much worse; sometimes rather acrid, like the remains of a bonfire, but sometimes almost as sweet as leafmould or good compost. However the plastic bags that clung to the bushes and trees along the track were less acceptable: shapeless great blue or red or purple blobs desecrating the bare winter branches.

Beyond the tip was a former gravel pit that had become a little lake, and had attracted tufted duck and coots, as well as the gulls that were investigating the rubbish. At Appleford Crossing my route swung to the left, along a dirty track that was being used by a constant stream of heavy lorries on their way to the tip. Bizarrely, at one point I had to step aside for a street-cleaning vehicle that was carefully sweeping the cleanest part, the centre of the track, stiff brushes rotating assiduously while the driver steered well clear of the high ridges of dried mud on either side, which looked as though a snowplough had come through, doing an extra shift as a mudplough.

Further on again, a Waste Management works was producing acres of mud as a by-product, and the track became increasingly revolting, though fortunately as yet it was a relatively thin layer over a good hard foundation.

My mother used to say, when out walking, that my father could find mud in the Sahara desert; and Ishbel likes to repeat this accusation about me, but today I had excelled myself. The very last section of chocolate-coloured gloop turned out deeper than the rest, and as the mud closed over my insteps, disgust was tempered by the thought that at least Ishbel wasn't with me. I could not imagine what she would have said about that mud, but it would not have been encouraging to hear, and it would all have been my fault.

Finally I was free of the mudscape, and gratefully walking along a pleasant farmland track bordered by low bushes. Once this had been more of a highway than a byway, for it was known as the Old Wallingford Road. In John Leland's day, it was still the main London to Gloucester road, and he came this way to Abingdon on his itinerary. The cry of a buzzard sounded ahead; it was perched on a telegraph pole near enough to take a photo, and glided heavily ahead of me to another convenient perch. Further off, a red kite swooped down to snatch something from under the nose of a startled gull. The village of Sutton Courtenay was visible beyond a ploughed field, and a well-trodden path turned towards it, the continuation of the alternative route nearer the power station, which I probably should have taken.

As the path entered the village, it ran between high evergreen hedges, arriving suddenly at a fork that offered a choice of similar paths. The map showed that the left fork led to the church, so I followed it, mourning an abundant apple crop that was going to waste in the adjacent garden, the ground covered with a great swathe of red and yellow rotting away, that could have made jam or chutney even if the apples weren't good eaters. We had four apple trees in the garden when I was a boy (our housing estate was in a former orchard), and my mother let barely a single apple escape; they were all stewed at the end of the autumn and stored in sealed Kilner jars in the loft, where they lasted us till the following harvest. She would have been furious at this prodigal lack of management.

The path emerged to give a good view of All Saints church, with its unusual two-storey brick porch prominent, and I was glad for once to have time for a look inside. Before entering I checked my footwear; happily, horrible as the mud had appeared, it had flowed off as easily as it had flowed on, leaving the trainers a rather different colour, but without the sticky detritus that arable mud can leave.

The church was well worth looking round: like so many country churches, an amalgam of styles from many different periods that somehow managed to be an intriguing blend without clashes. In All Saints, this blend included parts built from the 12th century onwards. The church guidebook explained that the brick porch had been built with money bequeathed in 1465 by Bishop Thomas Bekynton, who had been Rector here, though the porch was not built till some decades after the bishop died. Perhaps it took the parishioners a long time to decide how best to use the legacy to improve their church; just the kind of issue that can lead to bitter disputes. One could imagine them debating the merits of a single-storey stone porch that would better match the church, as opposed to two storeys of brick that would offer more usefulness for the same money.

Taunt said of All Saints that 'the interior sadly wants general restoration'; clearly something had been done since, for it looked in good order. On the west wall was a long list of incumbents: I recognised the name Tiptaft. William Tiptaft preached here for only three years, but during that time he had a considerable effect locally:

> The church soon became so filled that there was scarcely standing-room in the aisles. And of whom was the congregation made up? Almost wholly of poor men and women. Labourers were there in their smock-frocks and week-day clothes almost as if they had just come out of their fields, poor women in their cotton shawls, with a sprinkling of better-dressed people in the pews; but a thorough plain and rustic assembly had gathered together to hear a sermon on the week-day evening – an event which had probably not occurred in that church or neighbourhood since the days of the Puritans.[1]

Tiptaft was described by a sympathetic writer, the son of his friend Joseph Philpot, as '…one who walks about most briskly on his Master's business… a very friendly and forthcoming person, …showing his emotions vividly upon his face, talking and gesticulating freely and easily, and soon striking up a friendship with those to whom he was drawn.' There was little now in this large, hushed, and venerable church, apart from the name on the wall, to recall the lively bustle of hundreds of churchgoers on their way in to hear the young preacher, or Tiptaft's resonant voice filling every corner with challenging words.

Out on the main street of the village, I wondered whether to take some refreshment in the George & Dragon or the Fish, but decided to press on the short distance to Culham, since the map marked a pub near the church there.

[1] Philpot, JH (1964) *The Seceders* Banner of Truth

At the corner, I crossed to the footpath to Sutton Pools, which led to the broad millstream, set about with stern notices warning against swimming. At first glance the water appeared calm, but actually there was a strong and swift current towards the thundering weirs. The illustrated warning BATHING AT YOUR RISK might have been the most effective, reminding the unwary of that most secretive of saurians, *crocodylus oxoniensis*, which gorges on drunken students in the immediate post-exam period, subsisting on the occasional fisherman for the rest of the year.

There were very desirable properties with gardens backing onto the water, and covered moorings. I heard the next day that one of the houses had been bought by 'that actress related to Asquith' – Helena Bonham Carter, keeping up a family tradition of living in Sutton Courtenay.

The path led round and over several weirs, set in a wide semi-circle. They dated from Victorian times: Taunt recorded that 'the weirs have been considerably enlarged in late years by the Conservators, who … have added to and augmented the waterway, so as to run off quickly the winter and summer floods.'[1] Now they were all in good force, as the Thames was full. From the far bank I walked across a wide meadow to the neat wooden footbridge over the Culham Cut, a broad canal built in 1809 to bypass a difficult section of river and include Culham Lock. Here I met the Thames Path, and crossed it to take the shortest route into Culham.

Emerging from the path onto Culham village green, I looked round for the pub, to see only the empty frame of what had been a freestanding inn sign. The former Lion Inn was now a private house, and there was no other pub in sight. I walked over to the churchyard, and wandered around some ancient gravestones. It was probable that John and Elizabeth Sexton, my great-great-great-great-great-grandparents, were buried here; many of the headstones were clearly old enough, but with age had come erosion and illegibility. I did not find them; and the church was locked – and little used, with only two services a month. I later found that in any case, this wasn't the building that they would have known; the old ninth-century church had been demolished and rebuilt in 1852, twenty years after John Sexton died.

He was a butcher, and I wondered whether he had traded here in Culham, or on the market in Abingdon, just a couple of miles away; or perhaps sometimes in Oxford. His wife was the daughter of John Sellwood, the Wolvercote blacksmith, and Oxford market would seem the most probable place for them to have met. I looked around the broad village green; some of the houses around it would have been here in his day, and perhaps he lived in one of them. If he wasn't teetotal, he might well have drunk his ale in the Lion, though in his day it was called the Sow and Pigs.

[1] Taunt, *op cit*

There are at least three different English tunes called the 'Butcher's Hornpipe'; John would hardly have known the later two, although published in his lifetime, for one is from Yorkshire and the other from Northumberland. But the oldest of the three, published in Playford's *Dancing Master* in 1718, before John Sexton was born, might have been played at local dances in his days. I have altered the key of the first and third sections to narrow the very wide range of the original, and make it playable on the D whistle.

Butcher's Hornpipe

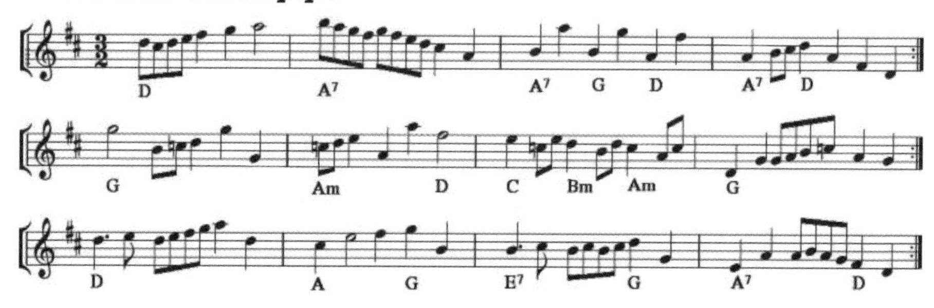

12th January 2012

I returned to the Culham Cut the following day, in the company of a Ramblers' Association party, the Vale of White Horse group on one of their 'gentle' walks. We had assembled in Abingdon market place, ready to walk upriver, along the railway, and down Thame Lane into Culham, where the Waggon and Horses (which I'd not seen the day before, being round two corners at the far end of the village) provided a good selection of lunches, as well as Hook Norton beer. If I had realised that the Springbok Stew was made with genuine springbok meat, rather than just being a generic name, I would have been strongly tempted. But the man who tried it said it just tasted like beef. Perhaps he didn't have too discerning a palate.

Before we set off, there had been some initial discussion among our predictably (on a midweek daytime walk) mature gathering:

'You need a back-marker if there are fifteen of us.'

'Do you want to be the back-marker?'

'No.'

'But you said we need a back-marker.'

'Yes, if there are fifteen of us, we need a back-marker.'

'I'm leading the walk. I can't be the back-marker. I can't be in two places at once.'

'No, you can't. But you need a back-marker.'

'Do you want to be the back-marker?'

'No, that's not what I said. I said we need a back-marker.'

The exchange continued for a score of turns, repeating itself at least three times, with increasing agitation on one side and a poker face on the other. Finally someone else volunteered to be the back-marker, and we were able to make a start.

After lunch, from the footbridge over the Culham Cut, I was again following my planned Four Points Ramble route, along the Thames Path until the cut joined the river. In the broad meadow by the path, a gigagaggle of geese, some Greylag, some Canada, grazed steadily.

'What do they find so interesting in the middle of a field?' asked someone.

'Well, I suppose it's like a small boy in a chocolate factory – or a boozer in a brewery.'

'What do you mean?'

'Grass – that's what they eat.'

'Oh. I never knew that. That is, I guess I never thought about what they eat before.'

'And it'll be good quality grass. Water meadows, that flood sometimes.'

The Goose and Gridiron

At a bend in the river, someone pointed out the Jubilee Junction, where the new course of the Wilts & Berks Canal began, the old course in Abingdon town centre having long ago been built over and obliterated. I heard a good deal about the proposed reservoir that Thames Water wanted to build: how enormous it would be, how massively high the banks around it would have to rise if sufficient water was to be impounded, how the canal would be routed round the reservoir with the water company's assistance, and how consequently the canal restoration people were all in favour, though locals still had their doubts.

One walker felt that the Jubilee Junction was 'idiotic – a hundred yards of canal going nowhere – who's going to use that?' Clearly he had no notion that the Wilts & Berks Canal would eventually be restored, and it was difficult to disagree too strongly when there was still so little of the canal in water, and it was so long since it had been abandoned. But I remembered the successful opening of the Rochdale Canal, and the Huddersfield Narrow, after decades of apparently absurd effort, when many at first were sceptical. The Kennet & Avon, re-opened in 1990, had looked unlikely for a long time. If the water company's scheme were to kick-start this end of the Wilts & Berks, then publicity and impetus might well result in further progress.

As we approached the Swift Ditch, which the Thames Path crossed on a stout wooden footbridge, I was asked whether I wanted to cross the old bridge, or look at it. I said I didn't mind, but was pressed to make a decision, and opted to stand on the footbridge and take a photo of the old stone Culham Bridge, which dated from the early fifteenth century. Pat Lonergan then persuaded me, and a couple of others, to double back and cross the old bridge after all. I was surprised at its breadth: two big Oxfordshire waggons could easily have passed each other in opposite directions. But there was a slight kink, resulting in a sharp stone corner on the east side, and it was understandable that a modern replacement had been built – nineteen-thirties, said Pat, who as a former Mayor of Abingdon knew quite a lot of local history.

The building of Culham Bridge in 1416, together with Abingdon Bridge and the causeway across the marshes in between, had brought a lot of trade to Abingdon. According to Leland, the bridges and causeway were completed in a single summer, by a workforce of three hundred, and the whole undertaking was stimulated by local distress at a number of drownings at the old ferry crossing.[1] Hearne wrote that 'the best artists that could be found were imploy'd, and every man had a penny a day, which was the best wages, and an extraordinary price in those times.'[2]

The Swift Ditch was an overgrown and unnavigable channel that cut off the big westward bend of the Thames past Abingdon. It had been dug, one walker said, to bypass the Abbey and its tolls; but I later found that current theory suggests that the Swift Ditch is the original course of the Thames, and that the present main channel of the river was dug by the monks (and, no doubt, a larger workforce employed by the Abbot) in the tenth century, to bring a proportion of the river close by the Abbey. In a thousand years since then, the latter channel has steadily widened, while the Swift Ditch has silted and narrowed from disuse, so that now one can hardly imagine that the whole of the Thames could have flowed that way.

Abingdon Abbey was revived in the mid-tenth century by Abbot Æthelwold, who arrived from Glastonbury, where he had been a monk under his friend Dunstan. For more than ten years they had been quietly reforming practice in Glastonbury, returning to the Benedictine ideals of poverty, chastity, and obedience. Now Æthelwold was to replicate this reform in Abingdon, where buildings were dilapidated, community depleted, and monastic observance almost non-existent. He tackled this with a hand-picked team of five monks, four of whom were later to become abbots themselves, so they were clearly selected for outstanding qualities. At the same time, Æthelwold was tutoring the future King Edgar, now a prince in his early teens.

[1] Smith, LT (1910) *The Itinerary of John Leland in or about the years 1535-43*
[2] Bliss, P (ed) (1857) *Reliquiae Hearnianae: The Remains of Thomas Hearne* Oxford

I asked my fellow-walkers if they knew that Edgar had been tutored in Abingdon, but no-one knew anything about that. I knew of King Edgar as 'Edgar the Peacemaker', who ruled for sixteen years with no rebellions, no raids, no wars or battles or even skirmishes: 'no host however strong was able to win booty for itself in England while that noble king occupied the royal throne', for potential enemies 'fearing his *prudentia* submitted without fighting'.[1]

'Kings and earls bowed eagerly to him and were ruled by him as he would'[2], not because he had proved himself in winning battles, like his uncle King Athelstan at Brunanburh, but because he had shown himself formidably well-organised, and he appeared to have the unanimous support of his people.

That support was any king's to command if he chose, for it was an age that prized loyalty greatly. But a harsh and overbearing king, or a weak and indecisive one, could easily strain that loyalty, and most other kings had to contend with rebellion or infighting among their underlings. Edgar seems to have been a man that others were happy to serve and follow, chiefly, perhaps, because he took the job seriously and did it well. He was diplomatic rather than overbearing, fair and just rather than arbitrary. But circumstantial evidence suggests he also had charm and charisma, for at the age of fourteen he was already chosen as King of Mercia and East Anglia, in preference to his elder brother who remained King of Wessex only.

So for two years this river ran as the boundary between the kingdoms of the brothers. Edgar was nominally under the overlordship of King Eadwig, but in practice he ran affairs north of the Thames, and when his brother died unexpectedly, Wessex confirmed Edgar as King, reuniting England under one rule. Already as a teenager, Edgar must have shown at least some qualities that gave grounds for these choices.

The detailed nature of his military preparations, his lawmaking, and his coinage reform, show a thoroughness and a drive towards completeness and uniformity that suggest a tendency to perfectionism. His support for monastic reform aimed at a different kind of perfection, and here it is said that Abbot Æthelwold opened Edgar's eyes to the beauty of the monastic ideal while they were together in Abingdon.

Æthelwold was clearly a man of great positive energy, who could carry others with him in his enthusiasm; 'busy benevolence' is the description of one writer.[3] Perhaps, while he was in Abingdon, Edgar learned something of how to lead a team so that everyone worked together willingly.

[1] cited in Wood, M (2010) *The Story of England* Penguin

[2] cited in Rex, P (2007) *Edgar, King of the English 959-75* Tempus

[3] cited in Robinson, JA (1923) *The Times of St Dunstan* OUP

Four years after he became king of all England, Edgar promoted Æthelwold (left) to the bishopric of Winchester, a key role in the royal town. Some have argued from the delay that king and abbot were not so close after all; but it is possible that the delay was at Æthelwold's request, so that he could complete his task of reforming and regenerating Abingdon Abbey.

As we walked across the meadows towards Abingdon, Pat talked of flooding, and how the last serious floods in Abingdon had not been caused primarily by the Thames, but by its little tributary, the Ock, which had less room to spread itself when overfull. The flat expanse we were crossing gave the Thames plenty of overflow potential, which was why these meadows, although fairly close to the centre of Abingdon, could not be used for overspill housing. This led on to a discussion of the difficulties of meeting central government targets for new housing in a town that was surrounded by green belt and flood plain.

As we came opposite the town, we had a fine view across the river of the attractive waterfront on the west bank. The original eastern end of the Wilts & Berks Canal was pointed out, as well as the fine almshouses alongside St Helen's church, and the old Gaol, built by Napoleonic War prisoners in 1811, and now converted, someone said, into expensive flats, whose thick walls and barred windows might give the affluent occupants a certain feeling of security. Finally we came to the bridge, where it was carefully explained to me that Abingdon Bridge is actually three bridges: Burford Bridge with its wide arch over the main stream, and narrow arches either side; Abingdon Bridge nearest the town, on the other side of Nag's Head Island; and Maud Hales Bridge, three arches over marshy ground further south, which also functions as flood relief. I was also reminded that the river had once been the county boundary; where we were walking, on the east bank, would have been Oxfordshire then, as it is now, while Abingdon itself, on the west bank, used to be in Berkshire, and had formerly been the county town.

Passing under a little arch to the right of Burford Bridge, we climbed to the road and crossed the two bridges to return to the Market Square. This was the end of the walk and time to split up, but four of us adjourned to the King's Head & Bell, where we talked politics and set the world to rights over some more Hook Norton bitter.

'Why the King's Head and Bell?' I asked. 'Was it once two pubs?'

'No idea. Never really thought about that. To us it's always been the King's Head and Bell.'

Five: Abingdon to Fyfield *(7 miles)*

Christmas address – ship sokes – royal oarsmen – Brewery Tap – Morris practice – The Curly-headed Ploughboy – Broom Dance eliminator – Ock Valley frost – Merlins – White Hart Hornpipe

12th January 2012

It would have been pleasant to sit indefinitely in the conservatory-style extension to the King's Head & Bell, learning about Abingdon affairs, taking in the ambience of the walled yard and the roofscape beyond. After all, I had plenty of time to kill; I had arranged to join the Abingdon Morris men at their pre-practice pint at 7.30. But the light was beginning to fade, and there were parts of Abingdon I wanted to see before dark, so I said goodbye and left, first strolling down to identify the spot at which I would start the next morning's walk, an alleyway next to the tall spire of St Helen's church.

A small white van stood near the church door, which was propped open, with dusty evidence of workmen coming and going. I slipped inside – it appeared the church would have been open anyway – and was taken aback at the unusually spacious interior. Taunt justifiably calls it 'magnificently large'. Instead of the usual two lines of arches, there seemed at first an uncounted regression of columns and arches, in a church that was much wider then it was long – at 108' the second widest in England, apparently. In fact there were five aisles of very roughly equal size and height, divided by four lines of arches, the result of successive sideways extensions adding capacity until St Helen's earned the nickname of the 'Great Church'.

William Tiptaft had been invited here from nearby Sutton Courtenay, to preach at Christmas in 1829. In this huge church, packed to the corners so that it held an estimated five thousand listeners, Tiptaft caused an immediate shock by starting the traditional Christmas evening sermon with the arresting statement: 'I stand before you this evening either as a servant of Christ or as a servant of the devil.' His intention was to force his listeners to agree wholeheartedly with him, if they did not violently disagree; he wanted no cosy indolent indifference. And although he started with a verse from the narrative of the birth of Christ, his theme was salvation by grace:

> As long as a man believes that he can do anything of himself to prepare his heart to receive grace or merit salvation, I cannot give him any present scriptural hope of being saved.[1]

[1] Tiptaft, W (2010) *Sermons of a Seceder* Gospel Standard Trust

Many of the listeners heard this message with joy; some of the congregation would have been his regular listeners from villages round about, who flocked to Sutton Courtenay to hear his preaching, and were glad that the doctrine of Grace should be expounded to a wider audience. But others were horrified; as Tiptaft wrote afterwards, 'the carnally-minded … were never so puzzled and confounded in their lives before.' Another clergyman, the following Sunday, took it upon himself to preach a counter-sermon, and then publish it, which Tiptaft welcomed as an opportunity to publish his own. The whole controversy led to the Bible, as well as the 39 Articles of the Church of England, being generally studied with most unusual interest. Tiptaft's opponent did not come out of this scrutiny well, being 'a wine-bibber, a great card-player, and a fox-hunter. They all acknowledge if I am not right, they are sure he is not.'[1]

Some of those Abingdon folk who were first jolted out of their complacency and into keen Bible study by Tiptaft's Christmas sermon would soon become members of his new independent chapel in Abingdon, after he resigned his living in Sutton Courtenay and seceded from the Church of England.

Beyond St Helen's were the long low buildings grouped in what Betjeman calls a 'paradise of almshouses'; I liked the oldest, the 15th-century Long Alley Almshouses, with their long oak-framed cloister walk and the tall lantern adorning the roof. They were built by the Fraternity of the Holy Cross, a guild founded by Henry VI and based in the church next door. According to Leland, they originally housed six men and six women.

From here I wandered down to St Helen's Wharf on the riverfront, and leant on the solid black rail to follow the progress of a coxed four: lean and fresh-faced schoolboys pulling strongly upriver against the current, while a motor launch cruised alongside, offering advice. Where the river narrowed at the end of Nag's Head Island, they stopped and began to turn the boat, letting the current swing them round, but disagreeing somewhat over how best to aid this process.

Watching the teenage lads manoevering their boat prompted thoughts of King Edgar. Part of his successful peacemaking, and a major reason why he was not continually pestered by Viking raids like his son Æthelræd, was his institution of three patrolling fleets, crewed by an elaborate system of 'ship sokes'. A 'soke' was an area of three hundreds, and the 'hundred' was the basic Anglo-Saxon unit of local collective responsibility. Each ship soke, no matter how far from the sea, had to provide one crew member for the king's navy.

[1] Philpot, *op cit*

Organised with Edgar's characteristic thoroughness, this provided a total of sixty ships, and over three thousand men, making twenty ships and a thousand or more men for each of the three fleets.[1] It is said that Edgar took part in one patrol each year, circumnavigating Britain by joining first his eastern fleet in the North Sea, sailing with them round to Devon, where he would transfer to the western fleet and continue with them to Man, before transferring into the northern fleet, who would take the king all the way round Scotland to the North Sea again.

It is hard to imagine Edgar doing this unless he enjoyed being on the water. He had been fostered in East Anglia, and might there have picked up a love for messing about in boats. In Abingdon, if his energetic tutor allowed him some time off, might he have borrowed a boat and gone out on the river, perhaps to catch fish for the refectory as an excuse for his excursion? It is tempting to picture abbot and prince taking time off together, seeking some quiet tree-shaded reach, enjoying God's created waterscape in a companionable silence that allowed them to hear the splash and cluck of a moorhen, or the song of a warbler among the willows.

Would the sturdy young prince have taken the oars, to allow his tutor to relax? Around seventeen years later, the defining hour of Edgar's reign came in a boat on the water, as the king of England and overlord of much of Britain was rowed on the River Dee, with six, or maybe eight, kings and sub-kings pulling on the oars. King Kenneth of Alba took an oar, it is said, with Kings Malcolm of Cumbria, Magnus of Man, Donald of Strathclyde, Iago of Gwynneth, and Iago's nephew Prince Hywel.

This might at first sound like a humiliation for the royal oarsmen; but knowing Edgar's gifts of diplomacy and team leadership, it is quite possible that the rowers were convinced that it was an honour to be chosen to handle an oar in the boat of so magnificent a king. 'Never since Arthur,' it was said, 'had any king such power.' In accepting the tribute of kings of Scotland, Wales, Strathclyde, Man and the Isles, Edgar was taking on responsibility for defending their territory as well as his own, and they must have been confident of his ability to do so, and to organise and command any joint force that might include their ships and men. Sadly, within two years of his crowning moment, this remarkable king was dead at the age of 32; and neither of his two sons, least of all the ill-advised Æthelræd, maintained his impressive legacy.

I strolled back through the town centre in the fading light. Old or even ancient as much of it was, not a single feature would have been here in Edgar's day, when the town and the abbey buildings were largely of wood. Now there was an interesting mix of styles and periods, including the dignified 17th-century County Hall with its high Renaissance windows, standing tall above its colonnade.

[1] Rodger, N (1997) *The Safeguard of the Sea: a Naval History of Britain* Harper Collins

Celia Fiennes thought it 'the finest in England, its all of free stone and very lofty, even the Isles or Walk below is a lofty arch on severall pillars of square stone … over it are large Roomes with handsome Windows.'[1]

The 15th-century Abbey Gateway blended well with the sturdy Norman arches of St Nicholas' Church, which was three hundred years older. Passing under the Gateway, I came to Trendell's Folly, a 'picturesque' ruin constructed from odds and ends salvaged from the ruins of the dissolved Abbey, but reproducing no known feature of the abbey as it had actually stood. A few ancillary buildings of the once extensive Abbey complex still remained: the Granary, the Checker, and the Long Gallery, but these were not open on a winter afternoon. There were interesting information panels along the Heritage Trail; I strained my eyes in the twilight to read about the fulling mill that had once used this millstream for power.

Finally I had to accept that the daylight had gone; sightseeing was effectively ended, and there were still more than two hours until my rendezvous in the Brewery Tap. Some of the time could be passed in a comfortable café with a large coffee and a thoughtfully provided newspaper, but eventually the time came for the café to close, and I took another turn round lamplit streets, pausing outside a pizza parlour, then moving on when I saw the prices, until I came to 'Friends', a little white-tiled takeaway with a couple of tiny tables in a corner, where I made a baked potato and sweetcorn last as long as possible.

At last it was time to stroll along Ock Street to the Brewery Tap. Ock Street has its own Mayor, elected by its residents in a traditional ceremony that has been kept alive by the Abingdon Morris Men. The Mayor of Ock Street functions as a kind of antithesis to the 'real' Mayor; he represents microlocal independence, defending the people against the politicians, and the west of the town against the north, as in 1700, when an ox roast in Market Square was followed by a tussle for possession of the horns, which the men of Ock Street won. The original three-hundred-year-old horns have been preserved, mounted on a carved wooden head, ever since; and now the morris dancers will only perform in public when the horns are present.

The Brewery Tap was originally attached to Morland's Brewery, which has been closed down since it was taken over by Greene King. Beer is still sold as 'Morland's', but Abingdon drinkers are not deceived; they know it has been brewed a hundred miles away in Bury St Edmund's.

When I was working in Oxford in 1973, at an early stage when I was still a temp placed by an agency, I visited Morland's Brewery to make a delivery, and got talking to a young man working there. I mentioned that I was thinking of changing my status

[1] Morris, ed *op cit*

and working permanently for the firm I'd been placed with, and he looked at me with a long face, framed by his shoulder-length hair, and said: 'Permanent job? Bad scene, man.' I wasn't sure then, and I'm still not sure now, whether he was joking or not.

Inside the Brewery Tap, I chose some bitter that *was* local: Abingdon Bridge from the Loose Cannon microbrewery less than half a mile away. It proved distinctive and well worth sampling, as I relaxed and read the Oxford area CAMRA magazine.

The fireplace was a marvel, set well back and high above the floor, in a broad brick chimney dividing the bar from a snug. As I sat, a pint of bitter on the next table, and a curved glass of mineral water next to it, were directly in front of the log fire, so that the flames danced in the amber liquid, and sparkled on the surface of the glass: a beautiful still life that was never still, but constantly moving.

With 7.30 approaching, I began to wonder if I would recognise the Morris men; I had been ready to look for a group of fairly mature men, built like beer lovers, probably mostly bearded, but the pub was filling up with folk that nearly all answered well enough to that description, and only when I overheard the word 'dance' was I confident that the half-dozen by the door must be the group I was looking for. I was introduced to Dave Spiers, the chief musician, who granted my request to play along at the practice, as long as I always listened to the first time through the tune before joining in – a very sensible request, since like any other Morris side, they played very familiar tunes in rather individual variations, and a visiting musician playing a different, or even the standard, version would not have been helpful.

We were soon in a church hall round the corner: a long hall with plenty of space for the dancers, sometimes in sets of six, sometimes eight, and even two separate sets of six still had room to advance and retreat. I was formally introduced to the Bagman, Tony Legge, and the Mayor of Ock Street, Roger Cox, and took my place at the end with the musicians, some of whom just played, though most dropped in and out, dancing and playing by turns.

They certainly did have their own versions of tunes; Dave commented that *The Curly-headed Ploughboy* was 'a bit tedious – only one A and a lot of Bs', but when the music started, his Bs were what I thought was the A music, and his A was rather different to what I would play as the B music. This is what I think of as the standard version:

The Curly-headed Ploughboy

The dancers worked their way through their repertoire, and I was able to join in the music most of the time. The Princess Royal, Constant Billy, and the Duke of Marlborough were all impressively executed, and seeing and feeling the dances on a wooden floor, rather than the usual outdoor flagstones or tarmac, gave a different perspective on the energy expended. They were well-grown, thoroughly-upholstered dancers on the whole, and when eight of them left the floor simultaneously, and crashed down again in weighty unison, fully half a ton of beefy manhood depressed the floorboards to a worrying degree. I had been entertained, browsing the Abingdon Morris website beforehand, by the spoof video showing one energetic dancer going into orbit round the moon; if any of these floorboards now gave way, they might see the first Morrisman reaching the centre of the earth.

After a few dances there was a pause, and someone came forward with a rather flimsy plastic broom, eliciting derisive comment; then a better one was found, then two fine broad-headed wooden ones, altogether a whole sweep of brooms, which were laid out head to head in the shape of a cross. Four dancers stepped up to perform the Abingdon Broom Dance, a recently revived traditional solo display of steps and leaps to and fro across the handle of the broom. After a minute or two one dancer dropped out, then another; but the two younger and clearly fitter dancers went on, the music meanwhile steadily accelerating, until finally one gave in, and the other took a couple of steps more to ensure victory, then collapsed in his turn.

'I was so glad you stopped then' he gasped.

It was time for me to thank the Abingdon Morris for letting me join in, and head off round the corner for a bus back to Oxford.

13th January 2012

The next morning was bright and clear, and my bus from Oxford brought me in good time for a prompt start, with the sun still low enough to hide behind buildings, and the air sharp and fresh. The Ock Valley Walk turned out delightful; a winding wooded path between two waterways, the Ock river and the millstream, though I was not at all sure which was which. The sunlight brought out the colours of the upper branches, while the path itself was still shaded. Birdsong filled this green corridor, half a mile long yet barely a hundred yards wide, and the canopy overhead gave the illusion of a forest journey, even though the houses left and right were clearly visible.

Before long, the path came out from under the tall trees; visible to the right were the ancient low arches of Ock Bridge, across which John Leland had entered the town on his 1542 itinerary. It looked the same vintage as Abingdon Bridge; in fact it had been rebuilt, rather than newly built, at that time, and parts of it may date back to the eleventh century. I used the pedestrian lights to hold up the heavy traffic on Drayton Road, and crossed to the frosty meadow beyond. The air seemed colder now without the tree cover, and I was glad to keep moving briskly, pausing only to notice a pink flower making a brave show of colour among the silver-grey frost. It might have been Round-leaved Cranesbill, or perhaps simply a garden escape, for there are winter-flowering geraniums.

As the Ock valley bent round beyond the furthest houses, I saw a wooden footbridge over the river; but the path did not lead that way, instead joining Mill Road past New Cut Mill – the 'new cut' presumably being the Wilts & Berks Canal that once ran here, which was new in 1810. Beyond the mill the path ran through fields, then up to, along and across the A34 Abingdon By-pass, the thunder of traffic slightly muted by the bushes and trees along the pathway. On one of the trees a buzzard perched, then flapped off heavily as I approached, repeating this evasion twice more as the irritating rambler kept coming too close.

I also saw several Merlins, but these were not swift little falcons, but big noisy chuntering helicopters making repeated circular flights to and from the nearby airfield. As the track descended again, I remembered the directions Pat had given me – the Vale of White Horse Ramblers regularly came this way – and took a slightly deviant route alongside the course of the old canal, here no more than a deep drainage ditch lined with thorn trees. Further on, it was not even that, but filled in and ploughed over, with only a line of telegraph poles to mark where the Wilts & Berks had once run. If the canal did re-open, assuming the proposed reservoir went ahead, it would run somewhat to the south of this old line, close under the high bank that would surround the huge new sheet of water.

The Wilts & Berks closed a hundred years ago, having struggled for a long time before that. After the Great Western Railway had run main line and branches all over the area that the canal served, there was much less custom for the slow waterway; and with less income, it was impossible to maintain the canal in good condition, making it even harder to compete with the railway. Already in the 1870s, Henry Taunt described the Wilts & Berks as 'in very poor order in places'. William Morris, too, criticised the neglect of the waterways, which he ascribed to the malign railway attitude: 'they would not allow the people of the country to use either the natural or artificial waterways, of which latter there were a great many.'[1]

The poet Alfred Williams, although he worked for the GWR as a hammerman in the forge, lamented the state of the canal in its last days: 'Here and there at the wharves may still be seen a few rotten old hulks, falling to pieces and embedded in the mud; the bridges are shattered and dilapidated and the lock gates are broken.' He contrasts this with an idealised description of the Wilts & Berks in its heyday, which he must have heard second-hand, for those days were over long before he was born:

> Then the long barges, drawn by horses, mules, and donkeys, and laden with corn, stone, coal, timber, gravel, and other materials, proceeded regularly by day and night, up and down the canal to their destinations – north to Gloucester, west to Bristol, east to Abingdon, and thence to far-off London. At that time …the channel was broad and free, and full of clear, limpid water …and the swallows skimmed swiftly along, dipping now and then to snatch up a sweet mouthful to carry home to their young in the nest under the eaves…[2]

I turned north, away from the vanished canal, to follow the path past the picturesque Marcham Mill, a fine whitewashed house surrounded by gardens that made the most of the River Ock and tributary brooks, altogether adding up to a price tag of over two million pounds. A lane led towards the main village of Marcham a few hundred yards away. Near an open field gate a heron stood in statuesque immobility, until I moved a hand towards the pocket that held the camera, at which it took off and flew over to the far side of the field.

Marcham was an attractive brick and stone-built village with plenty of signs of life; the pub appeared to be open mid-morning; a notice in a cottage window advertised a club meeting; pedestrians were passing. I was impressed by the two dignified terracotta lions flanking the steps to the old Village Institute, a building which sadly appeared to be uneconomic to run as a village hall, causing much local controversy.

To the west was All Saints Church, and the path to Frilford ran through the churchyard and down to a walled path alongside a tree-lined pool. At the edge of the pool, vivid red-stemmed bushes, probably dogwood, caught the sunlight. The morning was beginning to be milder as well as brighter, now that the sun was well above the horizon, illuminating the smooth grey trunks of tall beeches towering over the next length of footpath. I saw just a corner of the little village of Frilford, turning northwards along the main road for an uncomfortable quarter-mile dodging traffic, then west again through Frilford Golf Course. Ramblers were sternly warned against straying from the path, and the right of way was thoroughly marked out with a broad swathe of aromatic wood chips and bark fragments.

[1] Morris, W (1892) *News from Nowhere* Kelmscott Press

[2] Williams, A (1915) *Life in a Railway Factory* Duckworth & Co

It made for springy and fragrant walking, and well worth the extra care needed not to walk in front of any golfers. By the time I came out of the golf course, in the hamlet of Tubney, I was beginning to realise that the morning's walk would probably end at Fyfield, rather than my optimistic goal of Kingston Bagpuize. Although I had been moving at what seemed a good pace (it was too cold to dawdle), time was slipping away; afterwards I found I had underestimated the distance by two miles.

I looked carefully at the few houses in Tubney, as I walked through, for this was the birthplace of John Sellwood, the Wolvercote farrier who was the father-in-law of John Sexton, the butcher of Culham. John Sellwood's father (and therefore my great-great-great-great-great-great-great-grandfather) was also called John Sellwood, and was a yeoman farmer here. He married Elizabeth Badnell in April 1718. Some of the cottages I was passing might be older than that; but there was no way of knowing where the Sellwoods had lived.

The last half-mile into Fyfield was along the old main road, now superseded by a faster, straighter section, so there was no traffic to disturb brisk walking on a hard surface. The village was quiet, and apparently deserted; I was here at the wrong time of year to see what Matthew Arnold wrote about in the *Scholar Gypsy*: 'Maidens, who from the distant hamlets come / To dance around the Fyfield elm in May'.

The White Hart promised welcome refreshment, but appeared closed, yet a large sign saying OPEN hung on the door. I tried the handle to no avail, then a gesticulating figure appeared in a window, waving me round to the back. On my way I passed the very clear notice directing customers to the back of the pub, so I had to apologise for my doziness to the young Australian behind the bar.

The pub was well-warmed by a fine log fire, and in no time I was peeling off layers down to T-shirt level, and enjoying the historic ambience and the welcome rest after seven miles in two and a half hours. As I absorbed some Hook Norton and crisps, I realized that this was no ordinary pub; it had the look of a small manor house, with a two-storey hall beyond the bar, and strong stone construction. I later found that it had been built as a chantry Hospital of St John the Baptist, to house a priest and some poor almsmen, as a bequest of Sir John Golafre in the mid-fifteenth century. It was dissolved by Edward VI a hundred years later; St John's College acquired it, and were responsible for the 20th-century renovations that revealed the original walls and arched ceiling. It would have been well worth a visit even without the beer.

The White Hart Hornpipe

Six: Fyfield to Bampton *(11 miles)*

The innkeeper's daughter – The Marquis of Huntly's Reel – the Duke's gardener's son – Chimney meadows – old nameplate – Thames Hornpipe – no food and no beer – Banbury Bill

5th March 2012

I returned to Fyfield on a bright March day nearly two months later, and followed the old road, now happily devoid of traffic, the short mile or so to Kingston Bagpuize. It was fairly mild for early March, sunny with little white clouds scudding across the sky in a brisk north-westerly breeze that made walking a pleasure. I met an old man walking his dog, who muttered something about 'where's the summer?' Perhaps he was feeling the wind-chill a little; a day or two earlier it had been really warm. But as far as I was concerned, the weather was ideal for counteracting the warmth that steady walking generates.

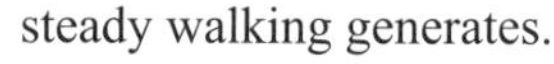

In Kingston Bagpuize I looked first for the church, which was soon found next to tall trees full of rooks' nests and echoing to their cawing. The poet James Thomson saw this as one of the classic signs of spring: 'the rook; who high amid the boughs, In early Spring, his airy city builds.'[1]

In the churchyard I looked for the grave of Alexander Murdoch, who died here in 1848; but none of the legible gravestones appeared to bear his name. One of the family sagas I heard as a boy, which I have probably by now garbled a little, for it was told to me a very long time ago, was my paternal grandmother's story of her husband's maternal grandmother, Jane Murdoch.

The story as I first heard it ran along the following lines: two young English painters and decorators, based in the Oxford area, gained a contract to do some work in a Scottish house, or hall, or mansion (no doubt my youthful imagination expanded and embellished even as I listened). While carrying out the work, they laid siege to and won the hearts of the two young ladies of the house, brought them back to England and married them, to the chagrin of their elder brother, who apparently refused to recognise an ordinary house painter as an acceptable brother-in-law. This brother was, apparently, referred to scornfully by my great-great-grandmother as 'Himself' or 'the Master'; she obviously had more sympathy for ideals of social equality, and considered his attitude snobbish. There was no mention of any father, so I assumed that he had already died, and therefore the elder brother had become head of the family.

[1] Thomson, J (1730) *The Seasons*

When genealogical information began to be more accessible via the internet, I decided to find out more about the Scottish connection, and contacted the Oxfordshire Family History Society, who made some very thorough searches, but had to apologise when it appeared that, as they put it, 'the story of the Sassenach workmen stealing away the Scottish heiresses has been a touch exaggerated.' According to their reading of the 1841 census, 'Jane does not seem to have had a brother and her father and mother were alive and well and keeping a pub in Kingston Bagpuize' – the pub in question being the Hind's Head, which is still there today. However the census did confirm that Jane Murdock, her sister Letitia, and her father Alexander, had all been born in Scotland, though Jane's mother, Jean, had been born elsewhere in England.

So the Scottish connection was genuine, and some further research showed that an Alexander Murdoch had married Jean Stringer on March 12th 1812 at St Martin-in-the-Fields, Westminster. Furthermore, a son had been born to the couple at the Lying-in Hospital, Endell St, Holborn, on 4th June that year, and christened William on 11th June. So there *was* at least an older brother, who by 1841 would have been in his late twenties and independent of his parents. Other children had been born to Alexander and Jean Murdoch between 1815 and 1824, all in Huntly, Aberdeenshire, showing that any stay in London had been temporary. I spent some time speculating on whether service in the army or navy during the Napoleonic War could have brought Alexander to London; but a subsequent visit to Huntly and searches in the town library gave a simpler explanation. Here my great-great-grandmother's birth was recorded more fully: 'Mr Alex Murdoch gardener Hy Lodge had a daughter by his wife Jane Stringer baptised & named Jane 28 Jan 1817'; and at her older sister's birth in 1815 he was also noted as 'gardener at Huntly Lodge'.

Some time between 1812 and 1815, then, he had been given the job of gardener at the residence of George Gordon, Marquis of Huntly, who had chosen Huntly Lodge as chief residence after his marriage to Elizabeth Brodie in 1813. It would therefore seem quite probable that Alexander had already been in the employ of the Gordon family, presumably at their London house in Belgrave Square, when he married in 1812, and had then been chosen to be part of the new staff team in Huntly, improving house and grounds for the newly-married noble couple.

Another employee of the Gordon household at that time was the fiddler and composer William Marshall, who worked as a factor, producing wonderful tunes in his free time. My ancestors would surely have heard him play.

The Marquis of Huntly's Reel, a Strathspey

The Marchioness Elizabeth was a keen horticulturalist, and ordered the Huntly Lodge gardens to be extended. She was also a woman with an increasingly fervent faith, who worked tirelessly to disciple her staff: there is a diary note in 1828 (by now she was Duchess of Gordon), '...began Anne Murdoch with Shorter Catechism, which she seemed to understand...' – my great-great-grandmother's older sister, who would have been twelve at the time.

The Duchess loved to encourage children in Christian study, and was charmed in an infant school, when the little one on her knee was able to answer her question better than the older ones. 'What does Jesus mean,' asked the Duchess, 'when he says, "Except ye become as little children, ye shall not enter the kingdom of heaven"?' The mite answered pithily, 'A little child kens that it can do naething its lane'[1] – that is, nothing by itself, the same point that Tiptaft and Romaine emphasised in their famous sermons.

I could find no clear explanation of how or when or why the Aberdeenshire stately home gardener should have become an innkeeper in the south of England. Perhaps his health eventually gave him problems working out of doors; by the 1830s he was probably in his fifties, and apparently the winter of 1837-8 was exceptionally severe in Aberdeenshire.

After my session in Huntly library, wandering down a side-street, I noticed a solicitor's, Murdoch, McMath & Mitchell, and on an impulse went in to see if this might link with my Murdoch ancestors. It turned out that it did; the firm's founder in 1835 was William Murdoch, the duke's gardener's son born in Holborn, who presumably had shown himself a 'lad o' pairts', and been helped to an education and legal training. I was shown an old photograph of William, and the expression on my great-great-great-uncle's face made it easy to imagine the disapproval of this solid new-middle-class citizen for his sister's marriage to a workman. Equally I could now see the reason for Jane Weaver née Murdoch's scorn for her big brother – who did he think he was, a workingman's son, to look down on an innkeeper's daughter for marrying a painter?

Returning to the family story, presumably the decorating contract had been here at the Hind's Head in Kingston Bagpuize, and Jane's parents had made no objection to their twenty-five-year-old daughter's marriage; only the snooty solicitor brother, up in Scotland, took exception.

The Hind's Head was close by the church, still trading; but it was too early in the walk to pause for refreshment, and as usual I was behind schedule. Today the schedule was governed by the sun rather than the clock, for I would need to press on if I was to reach Bampton before dark.

[1] Moody Stuart, Rev A (1865) *Life and Letters of Elizabeth, last Duchess of Gordon* James Nisbet

I followed the long street that led through Kingston Bagpuize and Southmoor, two villages that are more or less one, admiring as I went the pair of red kites circling over back gardens close to the road, the white patches under their slightly bent wings very sharply visible.

I had another family connection with Kingston Bagpuize, for Thomas Sexton, the paternal grandfather of John Sexton the Culham butcher, had been born here in 1685, before moving to Culham and settling there. Thomas's father Robert, and grandfather Isaac, had also been born here, but his great-grandfather Robert Sexton had come from Great Coxwell, a little further west, and I would be walking through there at a later stage of the book.

Just before the Waggon & Horses, a path led away northwards, over the A420 by-pass, the high footbridge giving extensive views over the meadows towards the Thames valley. 'The north wind makes walking weather,' wrote Edward Thomas from a similar vantage point, 'and the earth is spread out below us and before us to be conquered.'[1] I was looking forward to exploring the villages and then the riverside. The footpath led down again, passing blackthorn trees in full bloom, to Longworth village, barely a mile away. This seemed a prosperous little place, full of well-maintained cottages with interesting individual details: a stone plaque on a gable end; a large annexe made of rustic planking; an ivy-clad inn, the Blue Boar, proclaiming itself 'Free at Last', under its sign that depicted the Earl of Oxford's part in the victory at Bosworth. The banner reminded me of walking past the battlefield, around 150 miles ago on the Four Points Ramble route. In 1485 it was noted with amusement that the blue boar had overthrown the white boar, symbol of Richard III.

At the end of the village was the church, on a low green hill overlooking the river in the middle distance. At first I thought the path went through the churchyard; then I realised it led past Longworth Manor, through a gateway adorned with a GWR loco nameplate from 7826, one of the 'Manors' that didn't survive, being cut up for scrap in Llanelli in 1965. Nine have been preserved, out of thirty built, but this dully patinated and weathered nameplate was, I reflected, probably half of all that survived of 7826. The other nameplate was doubtless treasured somewhere; such mementoes are valued at several thousand pounds each these days.

Although a completely Great Western design, 7826 *Longworth Manor* was built by British Railways in 1950, and spent all her relatively short life in Wales.

[1] Thomas, E (1909) *The South Country* JM Dent & Sons

Like others in her class, she received a small but very significant modification in the mid-fifties: a reduction in the diameter of the chimney from $5\frac{1}{8}$ inches to $4\frac{7}{8}$ inches, improving the draught to the extent of almost doubling the steam-raising capacity, turning rather feeble locomotives into excellent performers.[1] For complete success a steam engine depends on the ideal proportions of its design, which is why the best examples often look good, as well as performing effectively.

The track led past the manor house and stables, substantial in creamy Cotswold stone, and on to another pretty little village barely a mile away, Hinton Waldrist. Once again it was stone-built, venerable, and well-kept. Looking at the two tiers of dormer windows on the long slope of the Old Rectory's tiled roof, and at the church and houses round about, I could guess that period dramas might be filmed here without needing much modernity to be hidden or disguised.

Down to Duxford was unavoidably roadwalking, but it was a dead-end lane with little traffic. At first it went steeply down from the hill to the flood plain, passing through coppiced woodland before levelling off. I was happy to see daffodils in the hedge, yellow and orange reflected in the well-watered ditch below. Together with violets and red dead-nettle seen earlier, it was a reassurance that spring was well on its way, and that the countryside would grow steadily more colourful week by week. On some bare branches the lichen was bright yellow, almost orange, contrasting harmoniously with the dark green ivy above and behind. Quite soon I came to the signpost for the footpath to the ford. Beyond a thatched cottage a kestrel hovered, flickering wings occasionally pausing, then beating again.

Duxford is Dudochesforde in Domesday, and was a ford already in Saxon times, associated with a man called Dudoc. Today the river seemed quite full, and the ford looked as though it would be best tackled in chest waders, rather than just wellies or rolled-up trousers. I turned to follow the path along the south bank of the river towards Shifford. It was a narrow path, often rather muddy: a slippery, clayey kind of mud that was quite unsettling when the path went close to the water's edge. For all that, the riverside was beautiful, even though the willows and alders were not yet in leaf, and the reeds and rushes at the waterside were dull creamy yellow, rather than the fresh green they soon would be.

Half a mile on, I came to the Thames Path proper, and the high bowed arch of the footbridge to Shifford Lock. It was a relief to see the bridge, and be sure that I could cross the river, even though I had seen the bridge on Google satellite view, and knew that it was there. Crossing the arch, I passed the lock amid the roar of the weir, and continued westwards into relative silence, alongside the broad straight navigation channel, towered over by tall trees that would give good shade in summer.

The Shifford Lock Cut was constructed as late as 1898, to avoid the navigational difficulties of the southward loop through Duxford. It carried a considerable volume of water, which explained why the Thames at Duxford had seemed a relatively small river.

[1] Nock, *op cit*

Halfway along the cut, another footbridge crossed to the northern bank, and a notice board gave information about Chimney Meadows Nature Reserve, over 600 acres of semi-wetland on both sides of the cut, which was home to many species of birds and wildflowers. I wasn't passing through at the best time to appreciate all its glory, but the sense of peace and tranquillity was wonderful even in early March. Small birds twittered in the trees above: robins, tits, and finches; and away in the distance was the unmistakeable call of the curlew, enhancing the breadth of the open spaces. The reserve is managed by the local Berks, Bucks & Oxon Wildlife Trust, which is trying to encourage a wetter habitat than had been wanted when it was just farmland. They have been much encouraged by recent sightings of bittern and otter.

'Chimney' might seem a curious name; it comes from 'Ceomma's ey' or island. Many of the local place names and field names have this '-ey' ending, for the old subdivisions of the river made islands out of many pieces of land; the hamlet of Chimney itself stands a few feet higher, just clear of the flooding even in a wet year.

At the western end of the cut, I saw that the Thames was rather more substantial before it divided. The path was on soft green turf near the riverbank, raised above the meadows to the north; it was easy to see that a wide area either side of the river would have been marshy and often flooded, in the days before it was managed. Cattle were half hidden by the tall buff reeds and grasses and rushes of a field that is still called Home Russia, meaning the rushy island near the farm. Looking west, upriver, the sun shone bright on the water; looking back east, the river was a deep blue, reflecting the early spring sky. The sparkle of the sun on the river put me in mind of the Thames Hornpipe, a tune of dubious origin first published in Glasgow in Kerr's Merry Melodies. A later version appeared in America in 1883 as the Ypsilanti Hornpipe; but the earliest version is untitled in Kerr's first volume, dating from the early 1870s.

Its style is reminiscent of James Hill, the Tyneside fiddler; two bars in the A music are almost identical to the beginning of Beeswing, and the beginning of the B music is similar to his Gateshead Hornpipe. Kerr was familiar with Hill's compositions; at least six Hill tunes are in that first volume of Merry Melodies, so this may be another of his. Why it should have acquired the title 'Thames Hornpipe' is hard to fathom. Below is a B flat version, a favourite key of Hill's.

Thames Hornpipe

Upriver, the path wound away southwards until it came to the Tenfoot Bridge, a name that refers not to the span, nor to the height of the bridge, but to the width of the flash lock that was there long before the bridge, and after which the bridge was named. Here the course of the river bent back northwards again, and I was glad to feel I was making significant progress along this long riverside stretch. In terms of enjoyment, there was no reason to wish the path any shorter, but my legs were just beginning to feel the miles covered, time was slipping away, and the sun was getting lower.

The stiff brown finely-pencilled shapes of teazles and burdocks caught the sunlight. Underfoot I frequently saw small snail shells, spiralled in pastel shades of several colours, but all apparently of one species, perhaps water snails left behind by an inundation, perhaps just a pale version of *cepaea nemoralis*, the Grove Snail. Away to the right stretched the wide flat meadow at the western end of the reserve, Upper Baingey, which had once been communally farmed. The trees along the far end of the field looked a good half mile away.

Coming round the next bend in the distance, a woman gave a sharp and anxious command to her shaggy pale golden retriever, who sat obediently to have a lead attached. When we passed, it turned out that the animal was liable to no worse crime than over-friendliness, but the owner had clearly had embarrassing moments in the past with strangers who did not reciprocate her retriever's affectionate enthusiasm.

As the river bent sharply westwards again, a footbridge took the path over another channel, where a stream, called the 'northern river' in an ancient charter, ran past Showell's Mead to Berhtwulf's island and the rush island. Now sluice gates would allow the meadows to be flooded or kept from flooding, as the reserve management judged suitable. The Thames Path ran under hoary and gnarled willows, their knotted shapes contrasting with the tall grey poplars across the river, which here seemed quite full and deep.

Before too long Tadpole Bridge appeared, with its distinctive handsome single arch, and pierced roundels either side, now filled in. It would have been pleasant to pause for refreshment at the inn, but the sun was dipping ever lower, and although journey's end for the day was not so far now, it was necessary to keep going. Another kestrel hovered over a riverside meadow, and ducks paddled on the river, as I pressed on towards Rushey Lock.

From the lock, the path to Bampton was clearly signposted north across the meadows, bare willow branches just catching the last horizontal rays of the sun. Only two miles to go, and some hope of arriving in daylight, or at least in twilight. Away to the west another curlew bubbled and trilled, as I crossed a solid wooden footbridge over a broad drainage channel that would lead to the Great Brook, a parallel stream north of the Thames proper.

In the next meadow, a round pile of grey feathers showed where a pigeon had met its doom, probably at the claws of a falcon. I was looking for a right turn that should take me to the shortest of several paths to Bampton, and turned along a green track that was blocked by the tangled branches of a fallen elder bush. Clambering over with some difficulty, I soon realised – identifying each individual hedge, as you can on the 1:25000 – that I had turned right too early; so I had to clamber back over and return, reassuring myself that I'd only lost five minutes.

Back on the right route, little black-headed brown-backed tits twittered round the bole of a large tree; either marsh tits or willow tits, but I can't tell them apart. There were four thin piping notes repeated, the third lower than the others, thus: tee-tee-too-tee, tee-tee-too-tee, which is the classic sound of neither marsh nor willow tit, so I was none the wiser. But it was nice to see and hear them, along with robins and chaffinches, and to be confident that they had survived the winter. Even if there was another cold snap waiting to catch us unawares before spring was fully launched, it would not be cold enough for long enough to cause much small bird mortality.

My boots had been satisfyingly cleanish on leaving Rushey Lock, so I was disappointed when two hundred yards of arable field loaded them with more sticky clay than the previous nine miles put together. All the way through Shillbrook Wood I was looking for different ways of cleaning the worst off. Shillbrook Wood was only twelve years old, having been planted by the Woodland Trust at the millennium; but it already had some of the feel of woodland, and was criss-crossed with pleasant grassy pathways.

Finally, with the light almost completely gone, I was in Bampton itself and searching for the B&B, where in due course I was very glad to be offered a large pot of tea, and plenty of gossip about the village, a thriving community, it seemed, of more than two thousand.

The landlady was dubious of my chances of finding an evening meal, but suggested the Romany as the best bet; and before long I roused enough energy to head out in search of food.

The landlord of the Romany was a substantial figure, bespectacled, dark-haired and full-bearded, both hair and beard well-streaked with white, wearing a welcoming smile as he asked for my order. I had carefully studied the menu and specials board, to no purpose, since there was no food on Mondays – except small meat pies in a hot cabinet, one of which I accepted as the best on offer. I asked what was on the handpump.

'I've got no real ales on tonight.'

'No food and no beer?'

He smiled tolerantly. 'There's John Smith's.'

I ordered a half, just to wash the pie down. The only thing I like about John Smith's keg beer is the adverts, which are superb. In their excellence they form another example of Beer Marketing Inversion, a law I'd first proposed in Book 2. This states that the quality of its advertising is inversely proportional to the quality of any ale; really good beer needs very little marketing.

At least I hadn't had to invest much in the pie or the beer, and I resolved to move on as soon as they were finished, meanwhile watching the local lads enjoying their darts and pool.

Back outside, I walked back through the lamplit square and made for the Morris Clown, which would surely have decent beer even if it didn't have any food. According to a CAMRA magazine, it was a former winner of Oxford Pub of the Year.

The landlord of the Morris Clown was a substantial figure, bespectacled, dark-haired and full-bearded, both hair and beard well-streaked with white, wearing a welcoming smile as he asked for my order. I blinked and wondered if I was hallucinating. Surely the man could not have run out of the back of one pub, through back alleys, and into another, just to confuse a weary traveller? But no, focusing more closely, it wasn't the same landlord, and more importantly, it wasn't the same beer, but a fine selection, including a guest beer from Cumbria. I asked what was local, and was directed to White Horse bitter, which came from Stanford-in-the-Vale, just six miles away across the Thames.

There was an empty table in the corner, but the landlord said 'I wouldn't sit there, unless you want to play cards with these gentlemen,' nodding at some elderly customers at the bar, 'and I wouldn't recommend that.'

I found another corner, and watched the mature card school, bantering with each other and the landlord as they gained and lost a few coins of little value. Some dry roasted peanuts helped fill the hole that the pie hadn't quite, and the bitter was excellent: light, fresh and dry. The White Horse Brewery was only eight years old, but they certainly knew how to brew a good pint. Like the Romany, the Morris Clown had all the atmosphere of a locals' pub, cosy and garrulous, though the average age of the regulars seemed older.

Bampton has one of the proudest Morris dancing traditions, claiming five or even six hundred years of continuous history. There is only any solid evidence, however, for a little over two hundred years; and more impartial academic research has established that the Morris style of dancing spread from the court and city to the villages around four hundred years ago[1], so it seems unlikely that the Bampton tradition is much older than that. Their true claim to fame is that they were among the few Morris sides that were still active, indeed flourishing, when Cecil Sharp and others began the revival in the early twentieth century. The legendary Bampton fiddler 'Jinky' Wells (right), with his musical knowledge from three generations of family involvement, had a great influence on the development of the revival, not only in Bampton, but among all Morris sides that follow the Cotswold style.

Eventually disagreements caused a split among the Morris men, and from 1927 there were two sides; and in the 1970s, three. Some say three are still active, but if so, the third side is so secret as to be invisible. The two visible sides have ensured maximum confusion by adopting the rather similar titles of the Traditional Bampton Morris Dancers, and the Bampton Traditional Morris Men. On the Whit bank holiday weekend, they dance their way round the village, in any gardens suitable for the exercise, courteously avoiding each other. Below is a favourite tune from the Bampton tradition:

Banbury Bill

On the way back up the lane to the B&B, I was grateful for the very subdued street lighting in the village. It made for a cosy and mellow atmosphere, and it also allowed the evening walker to look up and see the stars: the Plough, standing up like a saucepan on its handle, and on my way down to the Romany the giant Orion had confronted me. Now, as the sound of the Bampton bellringers practising their change-ringing floated over the village, the moon behind me cast a stronger shadow than any of the streetlights round about.

[1] Forrest, J (1999) *The History of Morris Dancing 1458-1750* Univ Toronto Press

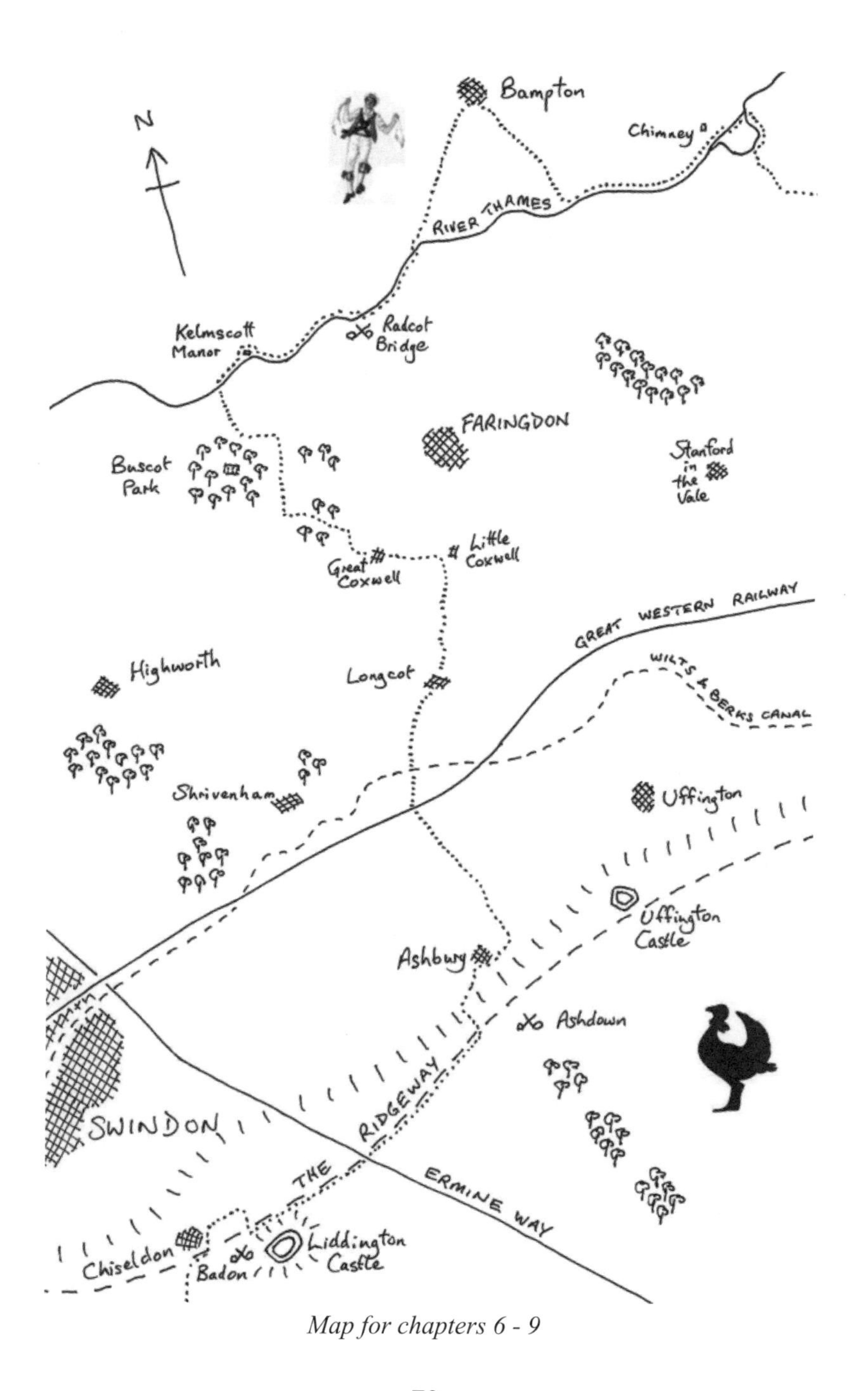

Map for chapters 6 - 9

Seven: Bampton to Hart's Weir *(6 miles)*

Unbuyable Grace – Country Gardens – Bunting obesity – Medieval treachery – changed riverscape – Kelmscott Manor – Blackthorn blossom – lamenting concertina

6th March 2012

The following morning I thoroughly enjoyed the traditional full English breakfast, which nowadays the English only eat if they've already paid for it and want to get their money's worth. Today at least, I hoped to be burning enough calories to justify the bacon and eggs, the mushrooms and the reputedly award-winning local sausage. Outside, it was bright and crisp after a clear night, and at first I was glad enough of a woolly hat and leather gloves, as I walked round to the church of St Mary the Virgin. It made a fine picture, its slender spire anchored with small and delicate flying buttresses to a sturdy tower. Inside was the usual happy mixture of periods, Norman pillars and Gothic windows together with Victorian renovation and embellishment.

An ancestor of mine came from Bampton: George Orchard, whose daughter Margery was born here in 1568, so George was almost certainly born in the reign of Henry VIII, and would have witnessed some changes in this church's services during his lifetime. After a few generations in Bampton, one descendant migrated to nearby Brize Norton; some generations later, another moved from there to Eynsham, where George Orchard's great-great-great-great-great-great-great-granddaughter Sarah Faichen was born, who married the Wolvercote blacksmith and ended up running the Red Lion there. So George was one of my 16,384 great-great-great-great-great-great-great-great-great-great-great-great-grandparents, and there are not many others of that huge cohort I can name even speculatively.

Margery Orchard 1568 - 1622 = **Robert Taylor**

John Taylor 1596 -

Katherine Taylor 1634 - = **William Wickens**

Robert Wickens *Labourer* 1656 - = **Dorothy** - 1705

John Wickens 1681/82 - = **Dorothy Denton** 1682 - 1751

John Wickins 1708 - 1787 = **Mary Crips** 1717/18 - 1759

William Wiggins 1746 - 1818 = **Sarah Payne** 1737 - 1804

Sarah Wiggins 1774 - 1843 = **Stephen Faichen** *Farmer* 1770 - 1818

Sarah Faichen 1802 - 1875 = **William Saxton** *Blacksmith* 1800 - 1848

He lived so long ago there was no point in attempting to look for gravestones or memorials, but hanging on a pillar was a translation of a document twice as old: William the Conqueror's 1069 charter, which granted Bampton and its lands to fund the upkeep of Bishop Leofric's cathedral in Exeter, a gift William hoped would gain him favour in Heaven, for 'it is a miserable thing that a king should be crowned in this world, and be delivered over to eternal punishment in the next!'

Leofric, one of relatively few Saxons to retain such an influential post under the Normans, must have been a persuasive man, to talk William round; and a duplicitous man as well, to dedicate his new cathedral to St Peter the Apostle, and yet ignore the words of that apostle to someone who thought he could *buy* God's free gift: 'To hell with you and your silver, because you thought to get God's gift through money!'[1]

Outside, the sun was a little higher and the chill a little less, as I walked through the village, appreciating the beauty and variety of its creamy Cotswold stone buildings. Close to the butcher that had provided my breakfast sausage, I found the footpath I was looking for, running in an attractive curve between a mellow stone wall and a green ditch, then over the Shill Brook, meandering among well-kept gardens that suggested another Morris tune popular here in Bampton:

Country Gardens

The path rejoined a lane that ran through Weald, a little outlying hamlet that was almost part of the big village of Bampton. Beyond Weald, a green lane ran on south-westwards, making very pleasant grassy walking between low hedges filled with birdsong, as the sun ascended the sky and the chill lessened. There were robins, a wren, and tits; chaffinches and possibly goldfinches; and a couple of yellowhammers, one of which posed obligingly on the hawthorn hedge.

Yellowhammers might seem common enough; I'd often heard them, and occasionally seen them, at every stage on the Four Points Ramble so far. But in fact their numbers have declined so much, and so quickly, that they are on the Red List of species at risk. They used to be *really* common: Bewick, in the early 19th century, says they are 'in every lane and hedge'[2], and the Reverend Morris agrees, 'there is not a hedge alongside which you can walk without seeing one after another flitting out before you'; and he refers more than once to 'large flocks'.[3]

[1] Acts 8:20
[2] Bewick, *op cit*
[3] Morris, Rev FO, *op cit*

Both writers note an alternative name, the 'Yellow Yowley'; and Rev Morris lists Yoldring, Yeldrock, Yite, and Skite among further dialect names.

When I was a boy, my grandmother told me (more than once) that the yellow-hammer always sings 'Little-bit-of-bread-and-*no*-cheese', and I often had the chance to listen and realise that, as always, Granny was right. Today, I listened carefully to this handsome bunting, as he perched on the thorn hedge and sang lustily, and there was no doubt that he was singing 'Little-bit-of-bread-and-*cheese*'.

Like the rise in self-indulgence, and exponential increase in portion size, among humans, it seemed that there was every chance of a similar loss of restraint, and degeneration into greed and consequent obesity, among birds, and soon there would be a need for more branches of Yellowhammer Weight Watchers.

In the field beyond the hedge, a number of fieldfares searched the grass for food. They come over from Scandinavia when the weather there is coldest, to forage in milder temperatures in the south of England. This year's winter was particularly mild, and the fieldfares were making the most of their winter break.

It was so mild, and the sky so bright and blue, that somewhere high up a skylark was singing, a joyous sound suggestive of summer, and an unusual combination with the sight of a flock of fieldfares.

It was good to be out and about enjoying so much promise of the coming spring and summer, 'when new-born March made fresh the hopeful air', as William Morris wrote[1]. A stile at the end of the lane gave a wide view of the grassy meadows beyond,

and small but clear a couple of furlongs away was the timber framework of Old Man's Bridge; although the Thames itself was invisible, its line could be inferred from the willow trees and the angle of the bridge. There was no discernible path over the green turf, but the bridge made a very clear landmark to aim for.

Coming close to the bridge, it was clear from signs that the Thames Path was on the far side; accordingly, I crossed, noting that its broad timbers looked relatively new. However the present bridge was apparently built in 1894. Originally there had been a weir here, Harper's Weir, across the top of which there had been a public right of way, and across which no doubt some of my Bampton ancestors had walked.

Within sight of Old Man's Bridge was Radcot Lock; as I approached, I recognised a reed bunting, perched high in a poplar tree, apparently enjoying the sun. This was a pleasing sight, for you don't see reed buntings every day unless you happen to frequent the right places regularly; until a few years ago I couldn't have identified one at sight. The reed bunting, *emberiza schoeniclus*, is a close relative of the yellowhammer, which can be more analytically described as the yellow bunting, *emberiza citrinella*. Buntings are members of the finch tribe, but bound together more closely by similarities in the shape of the head and beak.

At Radcot Lock a waterways worker greeted me with a comment on the glorious weather, and I readily agreed with him. It was ideal both for an outdoor job, and for riverside walking. I was glad to see a man enjoying his work; William Morris believed passionately that work could and should be a source of happiness in itself, rather than merely a source of money with which to try and buy happiness in the few remaining hours of leisure. He was well aware, however, that this ideal was seldom realised in his day:

> Be sure that … the blindness and hurry of civilisation, as it now is, have to answer a heavy charge as to that enormous amount of pleasureless work--work that tries every muscle of the body and every atom of the brain, and which is done without pleasure and without aim--work which everybody who has to do with tries to shuffle off in the speediest way that dread of starvation or ruin will allow him.[2]

[1] Morris, W (1868) *The Earthly Paradise* Ellis
[2] Morris, W (1882) *Hopes and Fears for Art* Ellis & White

Alfred Williams, the 'hammerman poet' and folklorist, who laboured at the forges in the railway works at Swindon, knew something of the 'relish' of work, commenting 'truly work is the salt of life, and physical work at that,' though he was furious at the way the foremen and overseers interfered with the potential satisfaction of a job well done, with continual pressure to increase production while cutting costs.[1] The Great Western Railway's desire to pay a good dividend to shareholders outweighed any concern for their humbler employees.

Today, at any rate, I had no employer trying to pressurise me. The Thames path continued along the grassy south bank; a few spots of yellow turned out to be the first celandines of the year, opening out to greet the sun. I was very briefly without a relevant map, because Old Man's Bridge had been in the bottom left-hand corner of one OS sheet, and Radcot Bridge was at the top of another, while in between, the Thames crossed so tiny a part of the bottom right-hand corner of a third sheet that I had not thought it worth purchasing, especially since I only had to follow the river, and could hardly get lost. Nevertheless it was vaguely unsettling to be 'off the map', and unsure exactly how far it was to Radcot Bridge. The view ahead, of the winding Thames with nothing but broad meadows and scattered alder and willow trees to be seen, gave little indication of any landmark. Far away to the south a curlew called, its piping note clear in the stillness; far off to the north a buzzard mewed; and close at hand came the loud irritable chuck of a moorhen.

Before long, boats and buildings became visible in the distance, and soon it was clear that this was Radcot Bridge, though for some time I had the clearest view of Canal Bridge, not realising that the original three-arched Radcot Bridge was away to the left. As I approached, a gaggle of Canada geese raised their honking voices on the far side of the river, while simultaneously wood pigeons and rooks were cooing and cawing respectively. Even so, the song of a vociferous wren was clearly audible through the competition. I climbed onto Cradle Bridge, which took the Thames Path from the south bank of the old course of the river onto the south bank of the new cut, and from the top of the arch I surveyed the peaceful scene of moored white cruisers and green grass.

[1] Williams (1915) *op cit*

Here on this island a battle took place, one which might be considered the first blow in the conflict that later became the Wars of the Roses. On the 20th December 1387, Henry Bolingbroke waited here to meet an approaching army. He would later become King Henry IV, although at this stage he had no reason to believe that he would one day be king. On their way south were 5000 fighting men under Thomas Molineux, Constable of Chester, accompanying Richard II's favourite, the detested Robert de Vere, newly created Duke of Ireland (left).

Bolingbroke was cousin to King Richard II, and like his father John of Gaunt, and his uncle Thomas of Woodstock, he was angry that the king put more trust in, and gave more honours to, a boyhood friend rather than senior royal relatives. Closer to the bone, de Vere had recently cast off his wife, another cousin of Bolingbroke's, and taken up with a low-born Bohemian lady-in-waiting. So there was a score to settle between two young men barely out of their teens.

Waiting at Radcot Bridge, Bolingbroke could be confident that his adversary would come this way; there was no other bridge for miles in either direction, and somewhere behind de Vere and Molineux was another force under Thomas of Woodstock. There were two bridges, either side of the island (the present straight canal cut, with its single-arched bridge, would not be built for many centuries yet), and the northern channel of the river was crossed by Pidnell Bridge. Bolingbroke had damaged or partially dismantled the latter; presumably it was less solidly constructed than the stone piers of Radcot Bridge. Now he could be confident that his enemy could not cross quickly or easily.

It is said that when de Vere arrived, and found the first bridge sabotaged and the second defended, he took fright and wanted to leave his force and escape alone. This lack of fortitude inspired the following scornful retort from one of the men under him:

> 'You made us leave our homelands; you talked us into putting our faith in you; you drove us to march here; so we're ready to fight and win alongside you, if that's the way it goes, or if things go against us, we'll manfully die with you.'[1]

But de Vere was not inclined to fight, and lightening the load for his horse by discarding some of his heavier armour, he attempted to swim the river on horseback. Finding himself a target for archers, he was forced back and into hiding on the north side. Darkness soon fell in the short winter day, and under the extra cover of fog, having abandoned the rest of his armour with his horse, he swam the Thames alone and disappeared into the south-west. His opponents, eventually finding armour and horse but no de Vere, believed him to be drowned, and this gave him the chance to escape abroad. In a curious postscript, he died a few years later at the tusks of a wild boar, or so it was said. He had many enemies.

[1] Walsingham, T (ed Galbraith, V, 1937) *The St Albans Chronicle* Clarendon

Meanwhile, Molineux was of a different metal: *vir dives et audax*, Thomas Walsingham called him, a wealthy and bold man. He and his men were fighters, rather than runners or swimmers, and they reacted to de Vere's flight by resolving to show that they could make a fight of it. But the river was in the way, and eventually Molineux too urged his horse into the water, at which Sir Thomas Mortimer, on the far bank, challenged him to come out or be shot with arrows. Molineux asked for the chance to come up unmolested, so that he could 'try with hand blows … and so die like a man'. As he floundered up onto land, however, Mortimer caught at his helmet, pulled it off, and stuck a dagger straight into his skull, which 'perforated his cerebrum', as Walsingham put it in elegant Latin.

According to the code of chivalry at the time, this amounted to murder, rather than legitimate death in battle, and some years later, Mortimer stood trial for his crime. His unchivalrous conduct might have been overlooked, however, if it had not been realised that much of the money to pay the troops that fought for Bolingbroke and his fellow-rebels came from the wealth of the Mortimer family.[1]

Once Molineux had been killed, the men under his command surrendered, or turned and fled. Few others actually died from the bite of steel at the Battle of Radcot Bridge, though it is said that many who fled the battle drowned in the marshes round about. Despite the lack of extensive slaughter, or any great deeds of valour, Radcot Bridge was a very significant victory. De Vere's flight, and Molineux's death, gave the barons the chance to humiliate the king in the new year at the Merciless Parliament, where Richard II was powerless to prevent some of his few friends from being executed for treason, and others exiled. This further hardened the king's attitude, setting him on the collision course that eventually led to Bolingbroke's usurpation.

The Thames Path crossed Canal Bridge to the north bank; then came a modern wooden footbridge over the side-stream that was all that was left of the north channel, the canal cut having taken most of its water. Boats clustered around the three low narrow arches of the original bridge, some of which, or perhaps even most of which, dated back to Saxon times. Upstream from the bridge was once again green fields, bare willow trees, and straw-coloured rushes, with no sign of human habitation for a long mile to Grafton Lock. There I was careful not to walk too close to a pair of swans, before finding the path through a cluster of boats parked high and dry on the bank. At the lock itself I took the chance to sit on a bollard, drink some water, and enjoy the tranquil willow-fringed waterscape.

[1] Saul, N & Given-Wilson, C (2002) *Fourteenth Century England vol 2* Boydell Press

The two miles above Grafton Lock, like the two miles below Tadpole Bridge the day before, were uninhabited, making for undisturbed riverside walking, with only the very occasional dogwalker or fisherman enjoying the unseasonably mild weather. More skylarks were singing, high in the blue sky over the wide green meadows. By now the early chill had been completely dispelled by the sunshine, and only the bareness of the branches overhanging the water, and the brown and cream colouring of much that would later be green, gave away how early in the spring it still was.

Coming to a smart metal gate, I saw the river winding back northwards across the green floodplain, and realised that Kelmscott was in sight. The view was hardly changed from the days when William Morris lived here, and brought his dreamt-of travellers up the Thames for the hay harvest in *News from Nowhere.*

> …the meadows widened out so much that it seemed as if the trees must now be on the bents only, or about the houses, except for the growth of willows on the immediate banks; so that the wide stretch of grass was little broken here.
>
> …a low wooded ridge bounded the river-plain to the south and south-east…[and they could see]…the flat country spreading out far away under the sun…[1]

Belloc, too, commented on how unchanged the scene was in his day: ' little is in sight save the willows, the meadows, and a village church tower, which present exactly the same aspect to-day as they did when that church was first built.'[2]

Modern research, however, has established that if you take a longer perspective on the Thames, the present single slow meandering channel is not the original or natural state of the river, but a result of many centuries of forest clearance, flood plain drainage, and river management for navigation. Before all this human intervention, the upper Thames would have been a river of many small channels, often swift-flowing over rapids, amid dense growth of alder and willow. Other reaches might have been slower and marshy, but also multi-channelled and thickly wooded.[3]

Approaching the village a little before twelve, I was glad to have made good time, but worried that lunch might not yet be available, or might not be available at all. Kelmscott was still 'a few grey buildings', as Morris described it, but perhaps not quite 'of the simplest kind'. You would need a secure and considerable income to live here. I wondered whether the pub marked on the map had been able to survive in such a small hamlet, and whether it was open at this hour.

[1] Morris, W (1892) *op cit*

[2] Belloc, *op cit*

[3] Robinson, M (2007) 'The Environmental Archaeology & Historical Ecology of Kelmscott'

Fortunately the Plough was still in business, open and welcoming and ready to serve lunch within a few minutes. Although I'd had the traditional full English breakfast at the B & B in Bampton, and so wasn't desperately hungry, I knew there was no alternative lunch place for several miles to come. Butternut, spinach, and goat's cheese tart sounded light and attractive, and I ordered it together with more excellent Hook Norton bitter. I preferred this to Piston Broke, a local beer from the Box Steam Brewery, which I might have tried out of interest, if its 5% hadn't been so much stronger than my normal preference. Hooky at 3.6% has become my most frequently sampled beer on the Four Points Ramble so far.

A footpath, at first enclosed by tall hedges, led back to the river, crossing yet another willow-fringed drainage ditch, which might once have been a secondary channel of the river. Coming to the Thames proper, another high-arched wooden footbridge led to my route to the south. Here I would cross the Thames for the eleventh and last time in this book, and the thirteenth time in all. I lingered for a little, looking upriver at a white splash of blackthorn blossom leaning over the still water, before saying farewell to a wonderful river, and setting off towards the midday sun. Blackthorn was one of many flowers that inspired a William Morris design, where he combined the little white stars with several other wild flowers that he would have seen within a short stroll of Kelmscott, though not all in flower in the same early season.

The footbridge, and the stillness of the water, were relatively modern; originally this was the site of Hart's Weir, a flash lock with a considerable fall unless the river was full, in which case boaters had to be careful; Henry Taunt recollected once 'when lying on my back in the boat to get through, scraping a fair amount of skin off my nose and face, through contact with the bridge whilst going under.'[1]

There was no sign of any waterborne traffic actually moving, yet once this had been a busy waterway. Even in Roman times, boatloads of pottery had been worked upriver, to be distributed to customers in the Cotswolds.[2] Two hundred years ago, 'between two and three thousand tons of Gloucester cheese were sent annually'[3] from Buscot Wharf, just upriver, most of which would have floated down to London, maturing as it went.

[1] Taunt, *op cit*

[2] Esmonde Cleary, AS (1989) *The Ending of Roman Britain* Batsford

[3] Bettey, JH (1986) *Wessex from AD 1000* Longman

Perhaps it was one of these cheese boats, returning empty, that Edward Thomas saw, out on one of his country walks in the area:

> Through the land went a dusky river, and in it a black barge with merrily painted prow. It was guided by a brown woman wearing a yellow scarf and she stood boldly up. In the midst of it a man played on a concertina and sang. The barge was light and high in the water; lonely and unnoticed, it threaded the long curves and still the concertina lamented and the tall woman stood boldly up.[1]

What could the boatman have been singing? Alfred Williams collected folk-songs in this area, and one in particular came from Jonas Wheeler, who had learned it at nearby Buscot Wharf from the boat people:[2]

In Brighton lived a fair young maid,
As fair as eyes could see,
Till a young man came a-courting her,
And proved her destiny.

She came to him next morning,
And wept most bitterly,
Saying - 'Willie, dearest Willie,
When will you marry me?'

'To marry you, Miss Polly,
Is more than I can do,
For I never intend to wed a girl,
So easily led as you.

Go home unto your parents,
And do the best you can,
And tell them your true love William,
Has proved a false young man.'

'I'll not go home to my parents,
Nor bring them to disgrace,
For I'd rather go and drown myself,
In some wild lonesome place.'

As Willie was a-walking,
Along the river side,
He saw his true love Polly,
Come floating on the tide.

He caught hold of her lily white hand,
And found that she was gone,
Saying - 'Lord have mercy on my soul,
I've proved a false young man.

Let none of my friends or relations,
Come lounging after me,
For on these cold and sandy banks,
I'll die with my Pollee.'

This is the kind of sad and sentimental song about misfortune long ago and far away that would cause the concertina to 'lament', and yet be a comfortably entertaining sound along with the ripples at the water's edge, and the creak of the tiller. Sadly, Williams collected only words, and no tunes; but the tune above, simple and with echoes of other melodies, would sound well on a concertina, and might be the sort of thing that Edward Thomas heard. It's adapted from a fragment noted by Frank Kidson.[3]

[1] Thomas, E (1906) *The Heart of England* JM Dent & Sons
[2] Williams, A (1923) *Folk Songs of the Upper Thames* Duckworth & Co
[3] Chappell, W (1893) *Old English Popular Music* Chappell & Co

Eight: Hart's Weir to Ashbury *(10 miles)*

Bull conflict – woodpecker harmony – Tithe barn – local Lollards – prayer from the heart – King William III – swift Stars – white beast – cover under elder – sanctuary in St Mary's

6th March 2012

From Hart's Weir I followed a gravel track southwards and upwards, away from the river valley. At one point the track ran between two fields that each contained a large black bull; both of these were bellowing from time to time, and one was moving about restlessly and rubbing his head against a post. It was predictable at this time of year; as James Thomson writes in 'Spring', when two bulls meet 'the bellowing war begins: Their eyes flash fury to the hollow'd earth.'[1]

I was conscious that only a flimsy fence protected me from one bull, and a single thin strand of electric wire from the other; not that they appeared at all interested in me. Although I knew that I was not necessarily in any danger, it still required a little nerve to walk steadily between the two; I was reminded of Mike Harding's definition of ramblers: 'honest, bull-fearing townsfolk'[2], and also of Pilgrim walking between the two chained lions. As the sound of bellowing receded behind me, the track continued past Kilmester's Farm to Taylor's Hill, where it was necessary to walk a couple of hundred yards up a main road – fortunately with verges – before coming to another southward farm track. Here I had to pause and enjoy the view across the lake that was part of Buscot Park, dotted with ducks and geese, and a Great Crested grebe.

The drumming of a woodpecker filled the space over the water, sounding as if it came from the trees just beyond the edge of the lake; but I could see no movement. A moment later it was echoed by a second, on a different note; and the two woodpeckers alternated drumming for some time. I listened, intrigued by the fact that the two notes were just a fifth apart, harmonising beautifully, except that the two birds didn't drum together. I would have dismissed this as a happy chance, if I hadn't heard the same phenomenon near Leighton Moss in Lancashire. Then, I had assumed that the different notes resulted from different resonances in the two birds' chosen branches, and therefore the perfect fifth was a coincidence. Now, however, I had to discard that hypothesis.

The only other explanation I could think of was that male and female woodpeckers (who would probably be courting at this time of year) normally drummed on different notes, and therefore the note was determined by some resonance in the bird's skull, rather than by what it was drumming on. This seemed more likely when I remembered that the bigger Black Woodpecker drums on a very deep note, which I once heard in Sweden, much deeper than either of the notes I was hearing now. Reminding Ishbel of this later, I liked her vision of barbershop woodpecker quartets recruiting Black Woodpeckers for the bass part.

[1] Thomson, *op cit*

[2] Harding, M (1986) *Rambling On* Robson

The fact that a woodpecker drums at all is remarkable, considering that the forces involved (deceleration of up to 1200*g*) in just one blow within the drumming are at least thirteen times more than would cause a human, or indeed another bird, to lose consciousness. The woodpecker has four distinct adaptations, not found in other birds: a more elastic beak, some spongy bone at the front of the skull, a skull bone with a special arrangement of cerebro-spinal fluid, and a hyoid, a strip of muscle tendon running from the tongue, under and round the back of the head, and over again to the top of the beak.[1] These four adaptations act together to dampen and absorb the deceleration, and thus protect the brain from the effects of repeated drumming. If woodpeckers did not drum, all this would not be necessary.

It would seem implausible that woodpeckers decided to begin drumming *after* realising that they had developed these special features; therefore the drumming must predate the adaptations; Darwinian theory predicts that the speed and power of repeated strikes would have gradually increased over millions of years, as the genetic modifications did their best to keep up. In this case we must honour the pioneer woodpecker drummers, as they toppled out of trees to lie stunned for a while before bravely yet erratically flapping back to their chosen hollow branch to try again, without any assurance that random mutation and natural selection would enable their remote descendants to drum without dizziness, nor any awareness of the future delight of passing humans who would listen to those remote descendants.

The idea that in fact the woodpecker's remarkable physiology is not the result of natural selection, but of some totally different principle or power, is of course not popular in the current scientific climate, but should perhaps be considered all the same.

Buscot Park was visible beyond the lake, and a month later Ishbel and I were able to visit and enjoy the fine house, filled with art collected by the first, second and third Lords Faringdon, the highlight of which was the 'Legend of the Briar Rose', by Burne-Jones, evocative paintings that ran all around the walls of the drawing room, in a setting that Burne-Jones had perfected while staying with his friend William Morris at Kelmscott across the river. We also enjoyed Peto's Water Garden, the long avenue framing the canal leading down to the lake, and looking across to the spot where I had listened to the woodpeckers. On the way down the avenue, we admired the unique fountain, with its figure of the improbably intertwined boy and dolphin.

[1] Yoon, S-H & Park, S (2011) 'A mechanical analysis of woodpecker drumming' *Bioinspiration and Biomimetics* **6**

Back in March, I followed the farm track due south, past Oldfield Farm, where I stood well clear of the track to let a huge tractor and trailer roar by in a cloud of dust. This was part of the Buscot Estate, and had once been the terminus of a narrow-gauge railway taking sugar-beet down to the brandy distillery on the river. In the nineteenth century Robert Campbell developed industrial agriculture here on a large scale, and this farm would have echoed to the hammering of blacksmiths, coopers, and wheel-wrights, as well as the screech of a sawmill, and the whistling of one of the little 0-4-0 locomotives, *Edith, Emily,* or *Alice*, as she pulled her string of wagons along the track. Sadly, Campbell's plans were on too large a scale to overcome market fluctuations, and most of his businesses ultimately failed.

From Oldfield I walked up a slight slope to Brimstone Farm, beyond which a clearly-signposted path ran east to the wooded hill of Badbury. Once inside the wood, the path ascended steeply, gaining over two hundred feet in the first really stiff uphill walking since the beginning of this book. It was good to be in mature woodland again; but soon enough I came to the car park by Badbury Camp, and was then heading downhill once more, with extensive views eastwards. Didcot Power Station looked disappointingly near, considering how many miles it felt as if I had walked since passing that landmark. I reassured myself that I had not come in anything like a direct line. The brick tower, Lord Berner's Folly, stood up sharp on its little hill beyond Faringdon. Closer at hand, a collection of small wooden jumps and obstacles in a little paddock were being used to train dogs in show-jumping.

The footpath descended steeply past a small wood, and then the great stone shape of the Tithe Barn at Great Coxwell came into view, a favourite sight of William Morris, who brought guests here from Kelmscott, and thought it 'the finest piece of architecture in England'. John Betjeman, too, fell in love with this enormous barn, and presented it on television, pointing out how the roof slates increase in size from top to bottom.[1]

I had a particular interest in this building, and had visited twice before, because my earliest known ancestor, Richard Sexton, lived and farmed in Great Coxwell, and this barn was a place he would have been very familiar with. It was built to house the produce of the village, for Great Coxwell was a grange of Beaulieu Abbey, and the crops were grown to support the monks there.

[1] Betjeman, J (2009) *Betjeman's England* John Murray

Will of Richard Sexton

In ye name of god Ame
ye xij day of deceber, Ao dini Mdlx quito

Y rycharde Sexton of great coxwell Sycke of bodye but hoole y mynde doe mak my last wyll & testamet yn forme & maner folowyng
fyrst and before all other thyngs y bequeth my sowl to god the father almyghte & my bodye to be buryed yn ye churcheyarde of great coxwell moreover y geve to thomas sexton my sone all my cattalles & allso all maner of other goodes yt y have both yn towne & yn Felde moveable or not moveable

and thys comendying my sole to almyghte god y do fynyshe my last wyll and testamet ye day & yere above named

records unto thys my laste wyll & testamet
john hycks of great coxwell arthure green
rychard dax viccar of great coxwell

Inventory of Richard Sexton

The ynvetorye of all goods & cattalls of rychard sexton of great coxwell

Inprimis sixe oxe / price		*iii*	*p*	*stud*
ij kyen / price	)			
a heyffer of on yere of age	)	*£x*	*1s*	
iij mars / price			*xls*	
wheet / barlye / & pulse			*xls*	
a lode of haye			*vs*	
a plow & on harow				
wt other thynges belongyng therto			*iiis*	
a bolster / a coverlet & too payre of sheets			*iii s*	*iiij d*
a table toord wt owt a cloth				*ii d*
iiij potts			*vj s*	*viij d*
ij pouces			*iijs*	
iiij platters & a saucer				*viij d*
ij barelles & a vatyg vessell	)			
a cadellstycke & a gledeyre	)			*xij d*
a knedyng iron	)			
ij coffers & an chere	)			*vj d*
a wold whytche				*viij d*

As a young man Richard was probably a lay farmworker for the Abbey, bringing grain into this barn, maybe later threshing and winnowing, all under the watchful eye of reeve or bailiff, who would be making sure nothing went missing. But in the 1530s, when Richard married and became a father, the monasteries were dissolved, and thereafter he farmed on his own account, doing rather well, if his will and inventory are anything to go by, although he owned no land.

In a few minutes I was inside the Tithe Barn, marvelling again at the ancient timber framing. Great wooden posts supported a fine oak roof, in a cathedral-like space. The complex cross-bracing of beams, crucks, rafters and purlins, constructed shortly after 1300, is apparently most similar to a slightly earlier Cistercian barn in Belgium; so possibly the Abbot of Beaulieu employed the same master-builder, recommended within the Order.

I wondered what music my great-great-great-great-great-great-great-great-great-great-great-great-great-grandfather (another of the cohort of 16,384) would have heard here in the village. The following, from Chappell,[1] was almost certainly already well-known by the sixteenth century:

Well-a-Day

The path out of Great Coxwell was down at the other end of the village, so I walked down the main street, noticing several fine old buildings, though probably none that would have stood in the days of Richard Sexton, until I came to the parish church of St Giles, which included much that my ancestor would have recognised. The timber-framed north porch probably looked as it would have when he walked through it, and the walls and roof of the tiny nave and chancel were little altered apart from redecoration.

Richard, together with his teenage son Thomas, would have been standing in this little church (no pews in those days) in the late 1540s, on the day when Cranmer's Litany was first read in English. I could imagine the impact on this middle-aged farmer of hearing John Chrysostom's thousand-year-old prayer in his own language for the first time:

[1] Chappell, *op cit*

> God, which haste given us grace at this tyme with one accorde to make our commune supplications unto thee, and doost promise, that whan two or thre be gathered in thy name, thou wilt graunt their requestes: fulfil nowe, o lord, the desires and petytions of thy servauntes, as maye be mooste expedient for them, graunting us in this world knowledge of thy thruthe, & in the worlde to come lyfe everlastynge. Amen.

The fluency and gentleness of Cranmer's prose would surely have penetrated to the heart, reassuring and strengthening the faith of the congregation. A few may have possessed English bibles already, for the area was known as a stronghold of Lollardry. William Berford, a carpenter in the village, was accused in 1499 of believing that 'indulgences from popes and prelates were without value', and was part of a group that met together and had access to the Scriptures in English.[1]

Richard Sexton was probably literate, given that he owned a pounce (the equivalent of blotting paper), and so may have read the Scriptures in his own language, and might have picked up the reference to Matthew 18 in 'two or three', which would hardly come across to ordinary farmworkers in the Latin: 'quique polliceris, ut ubi duo vel tres congregati fuerint in tuo nomine, te eorum supplicationes clementer exauditurum.' I wondered whether the minister in Great Coxwell at the time had been pleased or sad to leave Latin behind. Using English would surely bring him closer to his congregation, both to seem and feel less different from them. Would he have experienced this as a threat, or an opportunity?

There was no way of knowing, and it was time to go. From near the church, a paved footpath ran a short half-mile across fields to the main Swindon to Oxford road, where I could wait for the 66 bus.

17th April 2012

I returned to the bus-stop opposite a few weeks later, and took the traffic-free lane towards Little Coxwell. The grass verges were colourful with dandelion and celandine, the blue of ground ivy, and the creamy flowers of white dead-nettle. On the sunny side of the road an orange-tip butterfly flickered amid the green undergrowth; on the shady side, under trees were the little white flowers of alpine enchanter's nightshade, bright against the broad toothed leaves. As I made to take a close-up of the enchanter's nightshade, I realised that the camera had no battery. It had been recently recharged, and, I guessed, not replaced. I would have to take more careful written notes for the day.

The weather appeared much better than forecast, plentiful small high clouds in a blue sky, with a cool breeze. At the first corner in the lane, my route was clearly marked, a broad bridleway to Longcot. My initial plan had been to walk from Little Coxwell to Woolstone via Fernham and Uffington, ready to stop over in Woolstone before joining a West Wiltshire Ramblers walk the next morning.

[1] Thomson, JAF (1965) *The Later Lollards 1414-1520* OUP

However, the cost of accommodation for a lone traveller in Woolstone had been discouraging enough for me to investigate alternatives, and so I was to stay in the Rose & Crown in Ashbury for £20 a night less. At first I had simply thought of adding the extra two miles to Ashbury onto my original afternoon walk, but now I was suffering a little from a mild virus, and so the shorter direct route to Ashbury seemed a more sensible option.

The bridleway was a broad gravelly clay track between low hedges, clearly well used; I passed both a horse and rider, and a walker with a Jack Russell along the way. Reading the 1:25,000 map carefully, I saw how the right of way eventually diverged at a very slight angle from the track; and a stile and green signpost appeared on cue, confirming the route across a corner of a meadow, over another stile, to confront a thickly growing brassica crop between myself and the next waymarker. There was nothing for it but to go round the crop, which took me back to the track I had just left. So much for careful mapreading; I followed the track once more until it gave access to the last half-mile of footpath into Longcot.

I had hopes of a pub in Longcot; the map marked one, and for once I was ahead of schedule instead of behindhand. The train into Oxford had arrived a minute or so early, and I had walked down to the bus stop and almost straight onto the bus, half an hour before the one I had thought the earliest catchable. Taking the direct route to Ashbury would also get me there sooner than necessary, so a relaxing pause in Longcot seemed a good idea.

At first I saw no pub; the church looked worth a visit, but proved to be closed. Outside was a sad little notice warning that if any workmen were visible, they were probably making off with lead from the roof. Just round the corner was the pub, raising hopes for a moment till I saw that it was boarded up, in the throes of a very full renovation. It was called the King and Queen, which if the name was original presumably dated it to the time of William and Mary, sometime after 1689.

Arriving as part of the Glorious Revolution of 1689, William III of England was anything but a glorious king. Winston Churchill quotes the contemporary assessment of him as 'a low Dutch bear', but explains William's surly character as being due to his harsh background: 'fatherless and childless', he had had a demanding life of physical, political and military struggle, yet 'within this emaciated and defective frame there burned a remorseless fire, fanned by the storms of Europe.'[1] The Irish certainly considered him remorseless, after the Battle of the Boyne, and the Scots likewise after Glencoe; the English did not exactly love him, so how did so beautiful a melody as 'King William of Orange' come to be associated with this morose monarch?

[1] Churchill, WS (1957) *A History of the English-Speaking Peoples* Cassell

The tune was first printed in Scotland as 'Bonnie Charlie' in the late 18th century, but that suggests that the Young Pretender attracted an existing tune to himself; tunes are renamed after contemporary celebrities, rather than after long-dead ones, so the 'William of Orange' name is likely to be older. The more modern name in Ireland is 'King of the Fairies', and together with these different names go somewhat different versions of the B music, both of which are so lovely that it would be a shame to miss either. Below is a version that returns to the earliest recorded key, D minor, adding together the different versions to give a 48-bar hornpipe.

King William III

Lacking refreshment from the empty pub, I took a swig from the water bottle, sucked another honey-and-lemon lozenge, and pressed on. The bridle-way was once more clear and easy to follow, coming after a while to a small copse, full of the fresh green of spring. A butterfly crossed the path and settled on green leaves, displaying its intricate arrangement of yellow flecks on a brown background to good advantage. It was the first Speckled Wood I'd seen that year, and a very fine specimen, posing quietly for an unusually long time; I wished the camera had been usable.

Coming out of the copse, the path crossed a little stream, which was actually the infant River Ock, the other end of which I'd walked along in Abingdon; but I didn't notice its identity till later. From the grass by the path a small bird burst upwards, starting its continuous skylark song as soon as it had gained a few feet off the ground. At Old Wharf Road I turned left along the road, coming to two houses that were all that remained of a canalside settlement. Here the Wilts & Berks Canal went under the lane from west to east, and I had hoped to walk along the line of the old canal for the odd mile; I knew that the Wilts & Berks Canal Trust were intending to open up as much of the towpath as possible in 2012.

But just here there was no access; on the contrary, notices discouraging it. On one side of the lane the canal bed was still in water, well-grown with reeds and rushes, making a pleasant tiny wildlife sanctuary within the garden of the house that had once been canalside, and hopefully one day would be again.

I moved on to the bridge under the railway line, a piece of Victorian engineering very much still in use, for this was Brunel's main line from London to Bristol, built in 1840 and still carrying expresses today. Two whined past, as I sat on a convenient abutment with my back against a concrete post and took a break. A hundred years ago those expresses would have been hauled by Churchward 'Stars', light but fleet of wheel and beautifully engineered: 'lovely engines', Nock called them, 'immense favourites with the men on both sides of the footplate.'[1] With their four cylinders distributing power to two different coupled axles, they were exceptionally smooth-running at high speed. They were also strong: a 'Star' could handle fifteen or sixteen coaches, in the days when railway companies ran longer trains when more people wanted to travel, rather than using complex differential pricing to persuade passengers to choose less popular times. The trains passing now needed an engine at each end to move eight coaches, which would have prompted caustic comment from an old GWR engineman.

A hundred and fifty years ago, you could have seen Gooch's famous 'Iron Duke' eight-foot singles steaming by with the 'Flying Dutchman' at 70mph or more, steady and smooth on the old broad gauge. The careful civil engineering of the line, the breadth of the track that lent stability to the trains, and the precision of Gooch's mechanical engineering, gave the Great Western Railway its 'magnificent speed and stately carriage'[2], and the prestige of world record breaking speeds as early as 1848.

Shouldering the rucksack again, I walked up the lane past Knighton Copse, noting the white horse of Uffington, rather indistinct on the edge of the hill to the south-east. It is much the oldest of the many chalk-cut horses hereabouts; nobody knows how old it is, though it must be at least two thousand years old, dating from the Iron Age at the latest. But it could well be a good deal older still, and may not be a horse at all. The shape is so stylised, either by original design or by the blurring effects of continual recutting over the centuries, that it could be wolf, dog, or dragon for all anyone can tell today. Whatever it is, the white beast has become a local icon, used indiscriminately to sell beer or promote tourism; its fine lines adorning beermats, mousemats, and book covers. Even though he uses it for his own book, Hippisley Cox thinks it 'a curious and wan figure'[3]; yet Anderson sees it as a 'magnificent creature ... high, slender, and beautifully proportioned', noting the theory that it might have been the emblem of the Late Iron Age tribe, the Dobunni.[4]

[1] Nock, *op cit*

[2] Williams (1915) *op cit*

[3] Hippisley Cox, R (1914) *The Green Roads of England* Methuen

[4] Anderson, J & Godwin, F (1975) *The Oldest Road: an Exploration of the Ridgeway* Wildwood House

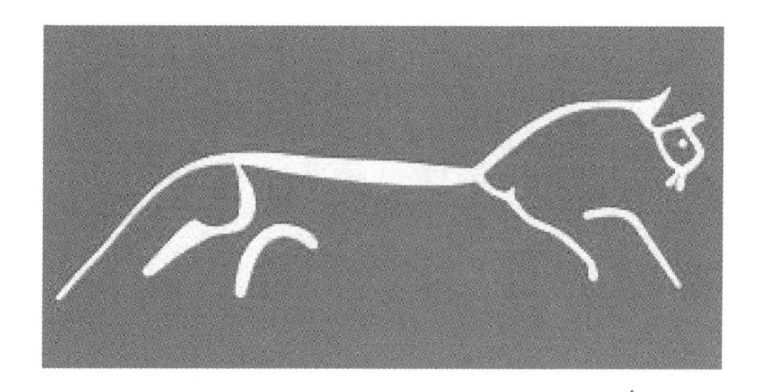

More recent archaeological investigation of Uffington Castle, the hillfort alongside the white horse, suggests that it was occupied in the early Iron Age, and not much used after that until Roman times.[1] The concept of a hillfort suggests warfare, defence against attack, but what evidence we have of the early Iron Age is of a people engaged in agriculture and trade, making the best of their lives in the task of survival. They were beginning to cultivate spelt wheat, which could be sown earlier, to give an early crop and avoid the hungry gap in the spring.[2] The pottery they used was produced on an industrial scale, not far away at All Cannings;[3] and presumably they traded their surplus produce for material goods, either through direct barter or some form of currency. The Ridgway, which runs past Uffington Castle, was primarily a trade route, and the forts along its length may have functioned as much or more as marketplaces, rather than pure strongholds.

Closer at hand, a pair of lapwing flapped here and there across a ploughed field. They used to be one of the commonest birds in the countryside, but fewer fields left ploughed for a time before sowing, and more use of pesticides, have deprived the lapwing of habitat and food, and now the rambler feels privileged to see lapwing. Richard Jefferies used to see many in this area, and was able to watch how lapwing, or peewit, appear to spend long periods flying for fun: 'Other birds fly for a purpose: the peewit seems to find enjoyment beating to and fro in the air,' he writes, they 'settle and feed again, and presently take wing and repeat the whirling about overhead.'[4]

I turned to follow a bridleway across a field of lush thickly-grown single-variety grass, which had clearly sprung up since anyone much had passed this way; it felt more like wading than walking as I made my way towards the distant stile. Through the next two fields, however, the bridleway was a broad, baked and bleached path that had been marked across a biofuel crop, using some sort of universal weedkiller.

[1] Payne, A et al (2006) *The Wessex Hillforts Project* English Heritage
[2] Cunliffe, B (1993) *Wessex to AD 1000* Longman
[3] Cunliffe, B (1991) *Iron Age Communities in Britain* Routledge
[4] Jefferies, R (1879) *Wildlife in a Southern County* Jonathan Cape

As I came nearer my destination, the weather began to look less friendly; some larger showerclouds were looming in the west, and I paused for a few minutes where a few trees grew at a junction of lanes and tracks. The nearest of the malevolent clouds was passing just to the south, attracted perhaps by the line of hills. Soon I was able to continue up the track towards Odstone Farm, observing on the way the white rumps of a couple of manically bounding roe deer, putting as much distance as possible between themselves and the passing rambler.

At the farm, there was a choice of routes: straight on through a herd of inquisitive bull calves, or turn left up a track to the main road. Seeing another shower approaching, which looked less likely to miss me, I turned left, hoping for some shelter further up the hill; and indeed, as the wind rose and the rain began, sanctuary appeared in the form of the footpath on the far side of the road, which ran under thick bushes, in what appeared to be an ancient hollow way, named on the map as Odstone Hill.

Dodging a couple of cars that swiftly hissed by through the rain, I found that the hollow gave enough shelter from the wind to put up the big golf umbrella. Ducking under two elder bushes, well covered in ivy, gave yet more cover as the shower intensified into a furious hail squall.

Although the worst of the squall soon passed, I continued sheltering for some time, and was rewarded by the sight of three long-tailed tits twittering in and around the thorn and elder bushes. In the end, lurking under bushes became tedious, and I ventured out onto the road, to walk westwards into a strong wet wind, holding the umbrella in front of me, which was less than helpful in seeing oncoming traffic, but kept out quite a lot of the rain.

Once it had abated, I lowered the umbrella and appreciated the view across the plain northwards. Coming to a line of cherry trees in blossom, I was reminded of Chiang Yee, the silent traveller, and how he admired cherry trees, and yet was made homesick for his native China at the sight of them.[1] He appreciated the visual effects of rain, as well, and might have enjoyed a walk on a day like this. I was beginning to be tired, and somewhat chilled, and was hoping that the Rose and Crown, where I was to stay that night, would not be closed for the afternoon.

In this I was disappointed, having first been encouraged by an open outer door; the inner was locked. There was a phone number that I could have used to disturb the landlord and gain admission, if I had had a mobile phone. But I had none, and have continued to resist the commercial pressure that turns every new gadget from an unnecessary luxury into a supposedly indispensable necessity.

At least one positive result of my mobilelessness was that the landlord could enjoy his afternoon break undisturbed. Meanwhile I needed to protect myself against damp and chill for a couple of hours. The nearby bus shelter offered admirable cover, but little of interest otherwise; so I walked up the lane to see if the church was open, and was pleased to find that it was.

[1] Chiang, Y (1944) *The Silent Traveller in Oxford* Methuen

St Mary the Virgin, Ashbury, was a curious-looking church from the outside, especially as the first sight of it was from a low vantage-point, so that the gable of the transept looked higher than the main roof, as did the large two-storey porch; while the tower at the west end was very short, yet broad and massively buttressed. The three features, transept, porch and tower, dominated and largely hid the body of the church. Yet inside, the church seemed reasonably proportioned, with an unusual wooden dormer window high above the crossing, letting in still more light on an interior that was already well lit. As in so many country churches, there were features from every period from the Norman onwards, blended in a mixture that did not clash at all.

I took my time looking round into every corner, reading the memorials and plaques, finding to my surprise that in 1777 the first ever Sunday School had been started in this obscure little village, by Thomas Stock, a curate with a rare gift of original thinking. Initially the school met here in the chancel, before moving to a more convenient (and no doubt warmer, in the winter) cottage nearby. In Gloucester, where Stock later worked, Robert Raikes helped him develop the idea into a pattern that was soon widely imitated; but it all began here in Ashbury.

I read of the six bells in the tower, the earliest provided by a Royalist churchwarden so that the church could celebrate the 1660 Restoration in what he felt to be suitably joyous fashion. A huge slab in the chancel recorded this gift in rough verse:

> To the memory of Mr William Phillips of the parish of Ashbury
> who dyed the 2 day of August Anno Dom 1684 aged 77
> And stopping here I heard a voice revile
> What no more due to such a sacred pile
> Can these be his just obsequies
> Who least a tongue should not suffice
> To huzza mighty Charles home
> Into his martyred fathers roome
> Himself hung up a bell to ring
> A gladsome entry to the King
> Distress nere made him leave king church or friend
> And growing riches made him grow more kind.

There was still a long time until the pub would be open, so I settled down in a pew near a window and read through a paperback that I had picked off a special shelf of second-hand books to share: Alister McGrath's *The Journey*, finding his reference to Ludolf of Saxony interesting. This was a writer I didn't recall hearing about before, and I determined to follow him up later. Ludolf's *Life of Christ* proved inspiring in its suggestion of using the imagination to place oneself alongside the disciples, or in the crowd, when reading the gospels, and so coming closer to Jesus.

The hours soon passed, and I was able to make my way back down to the Rose and Crown, and shed rucksack, coat and footwear before heading for the bar.

The Arkell's 2B bitter, light and refreshing, and the simple homely cottage pie, made very acceptable refuelling. Arkell's was a family brewery with 169 years of experience satisfying the palates of beer drinkers in the region around Swindon, and they were still expanding their estate; this Ashbury pub had been added in 1994. John Arkell the founder had returned from emigration to Canada, to be with the girl he loved; and his faithfulness was rewarded with commercial success when his new brewery coincided with the expansion of Swindon as a railway town. Labouring in the railway workshops was thirsty work.

I wondered if the Rose & Crown, in Richard Jefferies' day a hundred and thirty years ago, had been the kind of 'low public' house he describes as the preferred haunt of the agricultural labourer in this area, serving 'a rather dark beer with a certain twang faintly suggestive of liquorice and tobacco with a sense of "body", a thickness in it'. One could hardly imagine anything more different from my pale and clear glass of 2B. Equally the cottage pie was much safer than the curious mixture of foodstuffs Jefferies describes the village inn as serving: the 'coarsest' bacon; 'delicious' new-laid eggs; 'the strangest hodge-podge of pheasant and bread and cheese, asparagus and cabbage'.[1]

[1] Jefferies, R (1880) *Hodge and His Masters* Smith, Elder & Co

Nine: Ashbury to Oare *(18 miles)*

Damp prospect – burdensome birdsong – Battle of Ashdown – defence of mud – antiPelagianism – Battle of Badon – Dick's Maggot – Battle of Barbury – King Commius – Galloping Alice – too fast for Mum – the Resolution – early cyclist – West Woods

18th April 2012

Sitting at my solitary breakfast, enjoying the excellent bacon and eggs cooked by the landlord, I had a fine view of the picturesque thatched heart of Ashbury village, its roadside gutters running swiftly under a steady downpour. A bedraggled squirrel humped its way across the road, paused on a stone to shake itself, and disappeared behind the drooping daffodils.

To the north were two small patches of blue sky, appearing slate-grey through the curtain of falling rain. Any thought of joining the West Wiltshire Ramblers for their walk receded into the mists of impracticality; given that my throat was still sore, it made more sense to take the shortest way along the Ridgeway to Chisledon, from where I could get a bus on the first stage of the journey home.

The breakfast room, which was the bar that had the dining tables in, was of pleasingly irregular form, roofed and framed and furnished with old wood. Having already forgotten that the website described the Rose & Crown as a sixteenth-century coaching inn, I asked the landlord how old it was. '1587,' he said without any pause for thought. If the name was as old as the pub, the rose ought to be a Tudor rose, white on red; but actually various decorations and the inn sign used a plain red rose. The red rose generally symbolises love, and the crown is of course a royal symbol; for Christians they are Christ's saving blood and sovereign authority. But in heraldry the red rose and golden crown have seldom appeared together since pre-Tudor times, for the combination would be politically undiplomatic.

By the time I had packed up and left the inn, the rain had stopped, blown away by a fairly stiff cool wind; but I still couldn't face joining the Ramblers, now that a shorter walk had been decided on. I took the climb past the church slowly, and then followed what looked like a good path westward along the contour line, some way below the brow of the hill. It gave fine views northwards over the Vale of White Horse, and north-westwards towards Swindon, where a few of the larger buildings stood out as evidence of the size of the town. However it was also necessary to keep an eye on the path, partly because it was still damp and potentially skiddy, but mostly to avoid treading on the many long earthworms that were crawling about on the surface, temporarily flooded out of their normal habitat.

After half a mile or so, a path led up to the Ridgeway; I spotted a couple of goldfinches in a thorn bush as I passed. The Ridgeway itself was a broad track lined with bushes and small trees on both sides, giving cover to many small birds.

Edward Thomas delighted in old roads such as this: '…the high-hedged lane, where I see and touch with the eye and enjoy the shapes of each bole and branch in turn, their bone-like shapes, the many colours of the wood itself, wrinkled and grooved, or overlaid by pale green mould, silver lichen or dark green moss.'[1]

A succession of wrens sang their complex, but rather unvarying song to each other, as they staked their claim to possession of little sections of the road. A wren's song is a delightful sound to human ears, nowadays at least, and I wondered if travellers along this road two, three, or four thousand years ago had also heard wrens singing, and if so, whether they had also thought the song a delight to hear. Come to that, did the wrens enjoy their own singing? Supposing, I thought to myself, humans had to behave like this, and every male had to fill his lungs and sing 'This is *my* house, and *my* garden; these are my flowers and shrubs; so the rest of you can keep a respectful distance if you value your *lives*' – a thousand times a day? Would we not soon find it rather burdensome, even if singing is fun?

After the rain, the track had its share of puddles but relatively little mud, with the exception of a farmyard that straddled the Ridgeway and supplied rich loam in squelchy brown abundance. However it proved possible to wind a dryshod route past the hazard. To the right was a footpath and stile that carried a polite and well-argued notice asking dog owners to make sure that their pets were wormed, to avoid their parasites infecting Eastbrook Farm's livestock. It was a very fair point, but I suspected that the sort of owners that could not be bothered to look after their dogs properly would probably not bother to read the notice, and might well just say a few ugly words and spit, even if they did read it.

Along the Ridgeway were the creamy flowers of white dead-nettle, and here and there the yellow of cowslips, standing tall on their long stalks. Chaffinch, Yellowhammer, and Great Tit were all arrayed in smart spring colours, but female pheasants and a thrush wore their usual brown and buff. Skylarks were singing as continuously as ever, and I wondered whether the pauses for breath were simply so short that human ears could not perceive them, or whether the birds practised circular breathing like professional human woodwind players.

Somewhere on this high open plateau, in January 871, Prince Alfred of Wessex and his brother King Ethelred the First fought an invading Danish army that was advancing westwards along the Ridgeway. The King was still at prayer when young Alfred decided the time was right to launch an attack, and charged up the slope towards the enemy. The Danes were not only defeated, but lost several key leaders, and although there was more fighting as the year went on, their advance westwards was checked, and eventually they decided that Wessex was too tough a nut to crack, and settled for occupying the east midlands.

[1] Thomas, E (1909) *The South Country* JM Dent & Sons

Much later, King Alfred the Great showed bishop Asser around the battlefield of Ashdown, pointing out the lonely thorn tree around which the fiercest fighting had raged, and showing where he had charged 'like a wild boar'.[1] This could have been simple boasting, but what we know of Alfred's character suggests that it might have been the wry amusement of a middle-aged man at the energy and impetuosity he had been capable of in youth.

Nevertheless, it would have required great courage to go forward and engage the enemy, for he was not only risking death or wounds in battle, but a more terrible fate if he had been defeated and captured. Less than four years earlier, King Aelle of Northumbria had suffered the 'blood eagle' at the hands of the Norsemen, a slow death of skilled butchery where the back ribs were opened up and the living breathing lungs spread out in scarlet mockery of wings.[2] Only two years before, King Edmund of East Anglia had also been captured, tied to a tree and used for archery practice before being killed.[3] So in every way the position of leader was the place of greatest danger; but on this occasion the West Saxons had much the best of the battle.

It was said that the whole area was strewn with fallen bodies, a sobering thought as I walked along the near-deserted track on this peaceful April day. Somewhere along the way I crossed from Oxfordshire into Wiltshire; or in pre-1974 terms, from Berkshire into Wiltshire. The hills east of here had been the Berkshire Downs for centuries, and it would seem odd to start calling them the Oxfordshire Downs.

To the north of the track a considerable area was taken up with pig farming; numerous saddleback pigs were grunting happily, rooting around in large brown fenced-off rectangles of glutinous mud that they had created from the green downland. A number of crows hovered and swooped over the dark morass, which they clearly found much more attractive than the grass outside the fencing.

Dear Mr Four Points Rambler,

You show here an unbecoming lack of respect for pigs, crows, and above all, mud. Whence comes this unreasoning prejudice against mud? It is a glorious substance, a life-giving mingling of two primordial elements, Earth and Water, and wholly worthy of celebration rather than excoriation. As your good wife will testify, you yourself are irresistibly drawn to mud in your peregrinations, and therefore you ought to acknowledge its splendid qualities.

Yours sincerely, *Emmeline Crowe*

Crows can be over-sensitive sometimes; I had not intended any negative judgment, merely being struck by the contrast between brown and green, and the porcine and corvine enthusiasm for ground-level nourishment. Eastbrook Farm is proud of its saddlebacks, rearing them on an 'enterprising organic system'.

[1] Churchill, *op cit*
[2] Wood, *op cit*
[3] Blair, PH (1956) *An Introduction to Anglo-Saxon England* CUP

High on a hawthorn perched a plump sandy-coloured bird that seemed just a little larger than the average lark or finch or bunting. It was repeating rather monotonous, slightly metallic *tseep – tseep* calls, and I felt fairly confident that this was my first Corn Bunting; probably not the first I had ever seen, for they are not uncommon in this kind of open habitat, but the first I had been able to identify.

The Ridgeway ran over the shoulder of Charlbury Hill, reaching around 790 feet at the highest point of the track, then slanted down to meet a road under a stand of beeches. Walkers along the Ridgeway now had to be roadwalkers for a mile or so, and the road soon came to the Foxhill crossroads, where an inn had long stood, and was still marked on the map. Sadly, it was no longer in business as an inn. The innsign for the Shepherd's Rest still stood separately at the crossroads; but the painting was faded and flaked, though you could still see the shepherd's tall crook. The building that had once been a pub was now the freshly-painted *Burj* Indian restaurant, catering presumably to customers driving out from Swindon, rather than passing walkers or cyclists on the Ridgeway.

The scene was quiet and peaceful, a remote spot of no great importance today, but once it must have been busy, 'one of the great Dark Age road junctions',[1] the intersection of the Ermine Way, the Roman Road from Calleva to Corinium and Glevum, with the Ridgeway, well used by the indigenous population if not by the Romans. Here, in the year 429, Germanus might have preached as part of his mission against Pelagius. Germanus had come from Rome to counter the heresy spreading in Britain, for Pelagius' argument, that moral and upright behaviour was necessary to earn salvation, was attracting a lot of support.

Originally from Britain, on visiting Rome Pelagius had been shocked to the marrow by the licentious worldliness of many who called themselves Christians, but who had fallen into the trap of antinomianism, assuming that since Christ had died for their sins, it did not really matter how reprehensible their conduct was. In reacting against this, Pelagius fell into the opposite error, which ever since has been labelled Pelagianism after him, of not only exhorting fellow-believers to aim for the highest level of morality, but also implying that a failure to reach the highest standards could result in the loss of their salvation.

Pelagius had presumably not read Ezekiel 36, where God promises to take out the heart of stone, and insert a heart of flesh, a heart capable of love. The Pelagian approach was for the patient to be their own surgeon, to take out their own defective heart and replace it. Augustine, among others, saw the heresy in this, and was stimulated to some of his best writing in the counter-argument. But not everyone reads theology, and Germanus realised that, especially far from Rome, preaching in public places was necessary to educate the common people in a correct understanding of the doctrine of Grace.

PELAGIUS

[1] Wood, *op cit*

Germanus' strategy was to preach wherever he could gather a crowd: in market places, and specifically at major crossroads, so it is not impossible that he preached right here, perhaps paraphrasing the apostle Paul's rebuke to the Galatians by starting off: 'You foolish Britons!', and following that with a direct quote from the epistle:

> I would like to learn just one thing from you: Did you receive the Spirit by observing the law, or by believing what you heard? Are you so foolish? After beginning with the Spirit, are you now trying to attain your goal by human effort? (Gal 3:2-3)

From the Shepherd's Rest, half a mile of roadwalking led over the M4 motorway and up to a road junction. Here the long-distance footpath was signposted left and would then ascend to another Iron Age hillfort, Liddington Castle, now appearing a considerable bulk, rising to over 900 feet; but the more direct route to my destination was the road, which remained on this contour at around 650 feet, and was also marked 'Ridgeway' on the map. I felt no great urge to climb to the top, which showed how far my instinctive reaction to any hill had faded since I was a boy, though the virus played a part, and the very obviously approaching raincloud clinched the decision to take the shortest route. It might well be that this hill, looming up on my left, was the original site of the legendary Battle of Badon, in around the year 500, where King Arthur struck down hundreds of enemies, according to the annals. But although it is fairly certain that the battle happened, and that it proved decisive in ending the assaults of the Saxons for the better part of two generations, and although Liddington Castle is the best guess as to the site of Mons Badonicus, there is no certainty that the battle took place here, or that Arthur was the real leader, or even that he existed at all.

He probably existed; he might have been here; he might even have won a great victory here; but it was all uncertain enough not to wish to take a detour to a rainy hilltop. I headed along the road at my best speed, as the rain gradually became heavier, and I experienced Wiltshire downland rain, like the young poet Charles Sorley, out on cross-country runs from Marlborough School:

> And I look abroad again
> On the skies of dirty white
> And the drifting veil of rain.

It was blusterously evident that this was one of the 'large slow-moving showers' so accurately predicted by the BBC. The small slow-moving rambler was very glad to have a large slow-moving umbrella to interpose between himself and the inclement elements. Other creatures seemed unbothered by the weather; yellowhammers flew from bush to tree, and a skylark saw no reason to stop singing: a cheerful, feathered Gene Kelly. Occasional traffic swished past, but the wind was not so strong this time, and I was able to hold the umbrella upright enough to watch out for the cars. By the time I turned down the narrow lane to Badbury, the shower had moved on, leaving a damp freshness to the landscape, and a cool breeze to begin drying the trouser-legs.

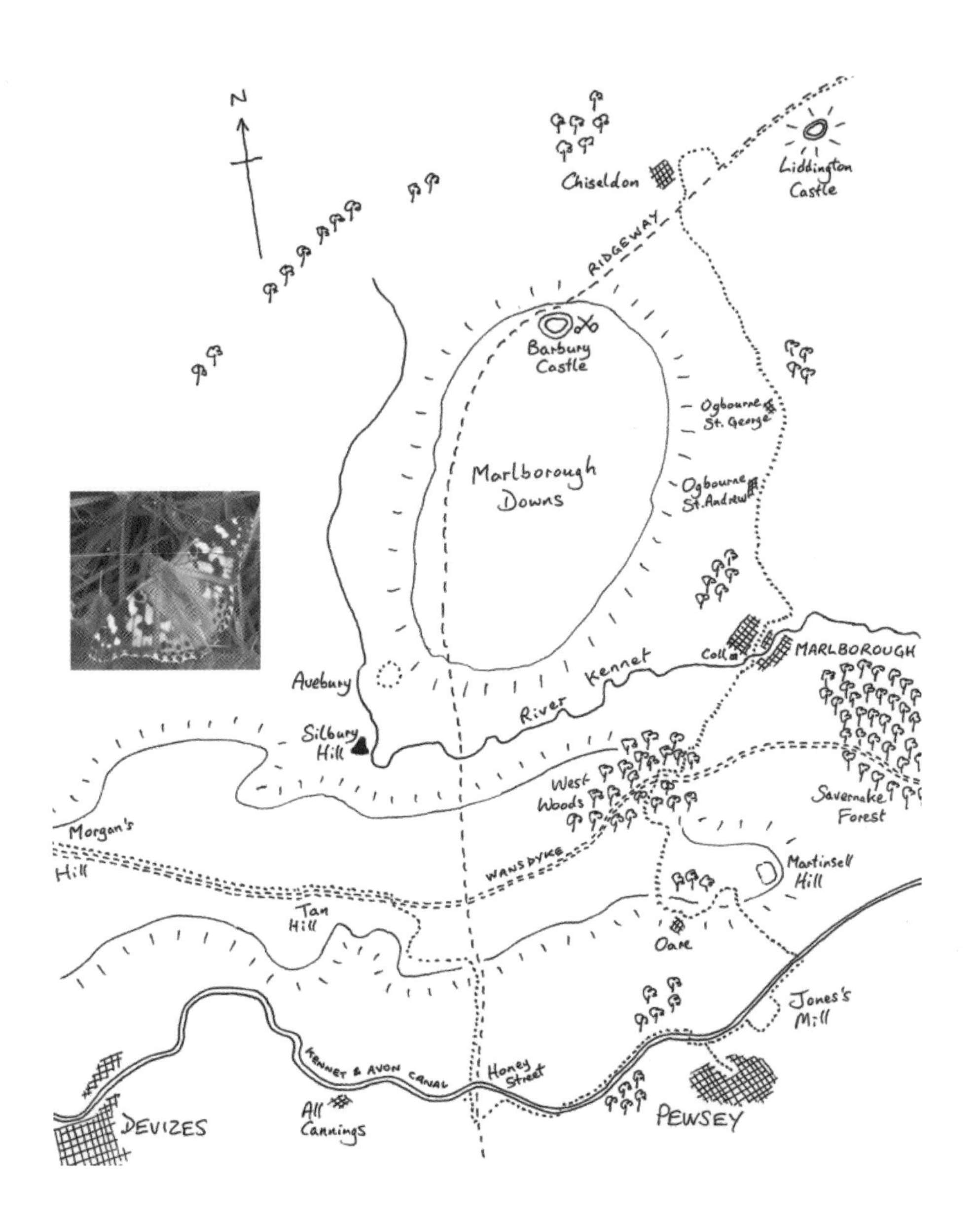

Map for chapters 9 & 10

The first sound in the quiet little village of Badbury was the excitable laughter of a Green Woodpecker; the second, the repeated *oo-OO-oo* of a Collared Dove. Some have suggested that these relatively recent immigrant pigeons are (like many international visitors) all Manchester United supporters, and are cooing *u-NI-ted*, *u-NI-ted*, all day long. I find it more interesting to assume that they are trying to hum the old English melody 'Dick's Maggot', but not getting past the first phrase.

Dick's Maggot

The lane out of Badbury soon came to the Swindon-Marlborough road. Across the road was the larger village of Chisledon, where I hoped to find a pub for refreshment, warmth and shelter; but it proved unnecessary to go into Chisledon. Glancing down the main road, it was a relief to see a board outside what was obviously a wayside inn, and moreover one that was open. The Plough carried a little rhyme on its innsign:

> With hopes we plough, with hopes we sow, with hopes we all are led,
> And I am here to sell good beer, with hopes to earn my bread.

I was glad to find that the beer was good: more Arkell's, of which I ordered some 2B again; and that there was soup available. After a cooked breakfast and a relatively short morning's walk I didn't want a full meal at this early stage, but leek and potato soup proved a warming restorative for a rather damp semi-invalid – though the sore throat was already beginning to clear up.

21st May 2012

I returned by bus a month later, and crossed over the main road to pick up the route where I had left off. A few hundred yards alongside the thundering traffic, thankfully with a broad pavement to walk on, brought me to where a walker could access the Sustrans cycle route southwards to Marlborough. The need to make public transport connections did not allow time to take a longer way round via Barbury Castle, thence to follow in the footsteps of Charles Sorley (left), who used to take cross-country runs in that direction, enjoying the worst the weather could fling at him.

I had thought, from the map, that Barbury Castle would at least be visible from the cycle track; but the lie of the land meant that only the shoulder of the hill could be seen, and I had to imagine the double rampart that was just over the brow somewhere.

Thinking about yet another hilltop fort, so close to Liddington Castle and Uffington Castle, I wondered whether they had all been built by the same tribe, as an integrated defence system for the Ridgeway (they all appear to date from the same period, around 600BC), or whether they were constructed by rival clans, each defending its own small territory. There is no definitive answer to this, but a suggestion that the period when these hillforts were built seems to have been one of population growth and pressure on resources.[1] So initially, they may have served as rival defence centres and focal points for quite small groups; later, as tribal organisation grew and groupings became bigger, they would probably all have come under joint control of whichever tribe was dominant at any one time.

Barbury seems to have been the most 'densely' and continuously occupied of the three hillforts,[2] and was the scene of a significant battle in 556, a couple of generations after Badon. Ceawlin and Cynric defeated a force of Britons, and this went some way to consolidate the beginnings of a West Saxon state in roughly the same area as had been controlled by the Atrebates. It has been suggested that the Saxon leadership actually took over a functioning Atrebatic state, rather than simply pushing all the British out and starting from nothing.[3]

Little is known for certain of Ceawlin, and still less of Arthur, who may or may not have marched or ridden and fought on these hills a millennium and a half ago; but another king who ruled here five hundred years earlier still, Commius of the Atrebates, is better documented, through the plain laconic prose of Julius Caesar's *de bello Gallico*.

Commius led an eventful life: chosen by Caesar as a client king in Gaul, he was 'a man whose courage and conduct he [Caesar] esteemed, and who he thought would be faithful to him'; he led a diplomatic mission to Britain on Rome's behalf, but later rebelled and fought against Rome under Vercingetorix. A treacherous attempt to trap Commius left him with a head wound and a lifelong aversion to all Romans; in the end he was allowed to move to England, where his vow, never to set eyes on another Roman, could be kept.

The bald list of Commius' adventures and changes of allegiance makes him sound a slippery character; yet he may in fact have had a very high sense of honour. At first he was probably impressed by Roman civilisation and style and apparent probity, and was happy to serve Julius Caesar; and the latter clearly trusted him implicitly, giving him a variety of responsible roles and challenging tasks on Rome's behalf. When Commius eventually joined the Gallic rebellion, there are hints that Caesar understood that tribal loyalty put him in a difficult position, and that he had to honour clan obligations.

[1] Cunliffe, (1991) *op cit*

[2] Payne et al, *op cit*

[3] Laycock, S (2009) *Warlords: The Struggle for Power in Post-Roman Britain* History Press

Commius' shocked reaction to the deceitful ploy used to trap him: 'and Volusenus, under the appearance of friendship as had been agreed on, had taken hold of Commius by the hand, and one of the centurions, as if surprised at so uncommon an incident, attempted to kill him...'[1] suggests that Commius had had such a high regard for Roman honour and honesty, which was then so deeply disappointed here, that he was as disgusted with Rome as he had previously been enthusiastic.

The Romans themselves may have been embarrassed at their treachery, since they 'indulged' Commius' stipulation 'not to be obliged to go into the presence of any Roman', and allowed him to go to England, where he established himself as King of the Atrebates, securely enough that his three sons followed him as kings, in a dynasty that ruled for several decades.

The cycle track, running south through this historic landscape, was broad, smooth, and pleasantly enclosed, lined with hedges or small trees that had probably all grown up since the time the railway was abandoned. Once this was the Midland & South Western Junction Railway, one of those fascinating straggling secondary lines that filled in the gaps in the railway system: in this case, north and south access to those Wiltshire towns that were primarily served by east-west routes. The line closed in 1961, having existed for around eighty years before that. Once upon a time the famous locomotive 'Galloping Alice' (left) would have trundled down this slight falling gradient, getting her breath back, having blasted up from Swindon to the summit at Chisledon. She was a purpose-built engine from Beyer Peacock in Manchester, low-slung, large-cylindered and small-wheeled, to be strong yet lightweight, able to haul heavy freight over the downs to the Southampton docks.

The old railway track made for steady brisk walking, the route ahead often visible for half a mile or more, the pale gravel line dwindling in a long perspective between, and sometimes overshadowed by, hawthorn and elder bushes. The green verges were embellished with constantly changing combinations of flowers: the white of cow-parsley ever-present, varied with the pink of herb Robert and campion, the blue of ground ivy, bugle, speedwell, alkanet, and forget-me-nots, the yellow of cowslips, buttercups, and celandine, and the mauve of vetch. A bushy green plant with small yellow flowers (left) was unfamiliar, tentatively identified as wintercress.

[1] McDevitte, WA & Bohn, WS (1869) *Caesar's Gallic War*

Further down the line the numerous white flowers of wild strawberry plants suggested a good harvest later in the summer. Other plants were not yet in flower; I recognised the leaves and young shoots of hogweed, meadow cranesbill, and rose-bay willow herb, while the broad fretted leaves of a large umbellifer that was not as far forward as putting out flower umbels were later identified as hemlock. In the shadier parts under taller trees, the purple spikes of cuckoo-pint, or lords-and-ladies, were just appearing in their asymmetrical sheaths.

All along the way, birds were singing: chaffinch, yellowhammer, wren and robin, and several more that I couldn't identify. I had a long stare at something that might well have been identifiable as a cirl bunting, if I'd only been a little nearer and it had been less silhouetted against the light.

At one point three very young cyclists came towards me at speed, the first two politely saying 'thankyou' as they whizzed past, though on that broad track I'd hardly needed to stand aside. The third and youngest, little legs pumping furiously to drive his small wheels fast enough, was calling 'Hi! Hi! Mum says "stop"! Mum says "stop"!' to his unheeding elder siblings. Some way behind, their mother came by at a more sedate pace, eyebrows down in an unamused expression.

For a mile or so, the route was just off the eastern edge of the map, so that I failed to register that where the track went under the main road and came up on the eastern side, was actually Ogbourne St George. Consequently, when I came to Ogbourne St Andrew, I assumed it was Ogbourne St George, and kept going, although I'd originally intended to take lunch in the pub at Ogbourne St Andrew. Only when I saw the housing estates on the edge of Marlborough, and the golf course, did I realise that, rather than being somewhere ahead, Ogbourne St Andrew was at least a mile behind me, and I was making better time than I had thought.

Ogbourne St Andrew was the birthplace of 'Phoebus', the singing sheep shearer David Sawyer, from whom Alfred Williams had collected many folk songs. 'You never seed a better songbook than I be, I warn,' was Sawyer's claim, which Williams endorsed. In retirement Sawyer lived near Williams, so that he was able to visit frequently and thus acquire all of Phoebus's repertoire. The following sample[1] shows that songs were not simply local; another version of this has since been collected in Yorkshire, and presumably it originated in a seaport somewhere. Details, such as the opposing nation, the names of the ships, and the relationship of the valiant damsel to the dead captain, differ in the various versions; some would have been updated for topical relevance as the song was passed around. The idea that the girl went to sea to be near her beloved may have been added for romantic effect; in other traditions she is the captain's daughter.

[1] Williams (1923) *op cit*

The curious anomaly that the name of the ship in the last line is different from the second verse may have some historical basis, for the *Resolution* was involved in the battle of Quiberon Bay in 1759, and captured the French ship *Formidable*, before herself running aground and foundering, so her victorious crew would indeed have returned home on a different ship. But it is totally improbable that all the details in a traditional folk song would relate to the same historical event, even if they might all have some historical basis. The tune was collected by Frank Kidson, and appears in Chappell.[1]

A story, a story I'm just a-going to tell,
It's of a young lady in London did dwell;
And, for to conclude, you quickly shall hear,
How she ventured her life for the sake of her dear.

So, now my brave boys, let's be loyal and true!
And after our enemies, for them we will pursue;
We shall soon overtake them all on the ocean wide,
And with the *Resolution* give them a broadside.

For with broadside to broadside, as far as we went,
To sink one another it was our intent;
But by the very first shot our captain was slain,
And the damsel in his stead was forced to remain.

We fought them for hours in battle so rare,
Till we scarce had a man that our ship could steer;
Till we scarce had a man that could fire off a gun,
And the blood out of each ship's side did run.

For quarter, for quarter, the Frenchmen did cry –
"You shall have the best of quarter," the damsel did reply,
"You shall have the best of quarter that I can afford,
That's to kill or be killed, sink, or jump overboard."

And now, my brave boys, here's a parting glass of wine,
And you can drink to your sweet lass, and I will drink to mine;
Here's a health to the girl, she's a girl of great fame,
She's on board the ship that's called *Newrion* by name.

[1] Chappell, *op cit*

At any rate, my original plan, to visit a pub that 'Phoebus' might have sung in, would have to be abandoned. Now it made more sense to press on into Marlborough for lunch, and I turned aside on a footpath through open meadows that looked as if it might go more directly into the town than the old railway track, which looped round to the east of Marlborough. The map marked no crossing of the River Og, but I hoped there might be one nonetheless – and there was, a concrete slab bridging the stream and leading to a little building that might have been something to do with water extraction. But it was surrounded with strong fencing, so the river crossing was futile, and it was necessary to go back and take a longer way round, along a suburban cul-de-sac of large detached properties, and down to a road entering the town from the east, past a beautiful reach of the Og, lined with willows and reeds and bright yellow marsh marigolds. Grey down was blowing off the willow catkins on the breeze.

The road led up to the high sloping square, a broad green facing south and surrounded by a miscellany of fine old houses, on one of which a blue plaque marked the birthplace of William Golding the novelist. He appears to have had little love for his home town, judging from his exposure, in *The Pyramid*, of what lay under the surface small-town respectability, 'so delicately poised ... so fiercely defended...' by an 'invisible line' between the different social classes.

An alleyway past the church of St Mary the Virgin led to a fine view of the Bear, (right) which turned out a very good place for a late lunch: a ham, cheese and mushroom omelette, salad and chips, washed down with Arkells 3B (last sampled in the Talbot at Eynsham in Book 5), since 2B was unavailable. 'People don't want the weak beer,' said the landlord, who clearly didn't share my enthusiasm for 2B. The lunch was improved by watching England's batsmen knocking off the winning runs against the West Indies at Lord's, and enlivened by overhearing the conversation of three old codgers who seemed to be personally acquainted with several famous football personalities.

I couldn't afford to linger too much in the Bear, and soon shook the stiffness out of my legs, to head down Marlborough's very broad High Street, lined with a variety of historic buildings, a scene which would have looked more attractive if it hadn't been jam-packed with 21st century cars and vans. It required a stretch of the imagination to picture Henry Wadworth the brewer, cycling through on his 1869 bicycle – even earlier than a penny-farthing – on his way home from London. By this stage he would have been tired but happy, commenting in his diary 'One hundred miles in 2½ days. I was one of the first to ride a bicycle down the Bath Road and I remember being pleased with the sensation caused.' He would have been sore, too, for the machine had wooden wheels with iron tyres.

Another blue plaque caught my eye as I passed St Peter's church at the far end of the High Street, and I saw that the future Cardinal Wolsey had begun his church career here, ordained in 1498. This would appear to be his only connection to Marlborough, for after his ordination he continued an academic career in Oxford, before becoming Henry VIII's Almoner, then Lord Chancellor, eventually founding Cardinal College, which changed its name to Christ Church after Wolsey's execution. Would the young cleric ordained here in Marlborough have settled for the career he was to achieve, accepting the ignominious end for the sake of the power beforehand?

I followed the road over the River Kennet, here pleasantly shaded by weeping willows and brightened by the yellow marsh marigolds at the waterside, and turned up the westward track beyond. Three teenagers, presumably Marlburians from their white shirts and grey trousers, overtook me, one walking springily on stiltlike blades that lifted him a couple of feet off the ground. What their purpose was I couldn't imagine. A galvanised kissing gate gave access to a steep grassy field, up which a visible path slanted. A brimstone butterfly flew by, pale yellow wings catching the hazy sun that was beginning to make the day quite warm. From the top of the slope there was a fine view back down to Marlborough, the 'little red-capped town', as Charles Sorley called it; the brick buildings of the public school standing out, closer on the left, then the two churches, further right, marking the extent of the High Street.

Marlborough School had a number of literary old boys; while Charles Sorley liked cross-country running to the north of the town, William Morris enjoyed rambling in these woodlands to the south. John Betjeman relished teatime at Marlborough, 'youth's most magic hour', writing of his 'enormous appetite' for 'marg' and 'jam and toast.'[1]

The path – marked on the map as 'Wansdyke Path', though the Wansdyke was still more than a mile away – proved easy to follow, past ponies grazing, buzzards circling, and a Speckled Wood butterfly posing, spreading out its yellow-flecked brown wings against the green undergrowth. I was able to get the photo that I'd been cross at missing near Longcot. An oak tree was coming into leaf, while a nearby ash was not quite so far on, prompting a review of the rhyme: 'Oak before ash, we shall have a splash; ash before oak, we shall have a soak'. I was never quite sure if this meant simply that it'll rain whatever happens, or whether a 'splash' is less than a 'soak', which would be bad news this year, when as much rain as possible was needed. At this stage in May, I was still unaware of how wet a year 2012 would prove to be.

The path wound onwards, over a stony field where the sun shone on odd white-flowered weeds that might have been whitlow-grass, and the bright light brought out the green tint in the white wings of a Green-veined White butterfly.

[1] Betjeman, 2009 *op cit*

Hedgerows on the approach to West Woods were full of bluebells, the white petals of stitchwort, and the nettle-like leaves and bold flowers of yellow archangel. The woodland itself was open, the tall slender trunks of beeches supporting a high canopy, so that the birdsong echoed as if in a cathedral. Coming to the rampart of Wansdyke, I turned along the path that ran along its ditch, happily not too muddy in this spell of dry weather.

The dyke made a good line to follow through the woods, until beyond Clatford Park Farm, where I took a more southerly line; a bridle path was marked on the map in the direction I wanted. But as so often in woodland, the tracks and drives that served woodland management did not necessarily coincide with the ancient rights of way, and although I was fairly sure that the broad track I was following went in roughly the right direction, I was not quite sure if it was what was marked on the map. The afternoon was wearing away. The woods were lovely: the birdsong all around, the wayside flowers and the smells of leafmould and resin. I passed a fine stand of wood spurge (right), tall in bright spring green.

However, the time remaining to reach the bus stop at Oare was shortening, and I was beginning to be anxious lest I went astray in the woods and so lost time. It was reassuring to see the lane to Bayardo Farm, though I had to cross some pathless wood to reach it; and it was then possible to stride out more speedily till some way past the farm, when on coming to a yellow field of oilseed rape, the junction of paths did not appear to reflect what the map marked. I took a best guess, and then followed a tractor track through the crop, becoming dusted with yellow from shoulders to shoes. By the time I reached the top of Huish Hill, and saw where the other end of the path came out, it was fairly clear I'd been a hundred yards or so east of where I should have been; but at least now I knew I was right again.

The view from the brow of Huish Hill was spectacular: across a great gulf to Martinsell Hill and Giant's Grave, where I'd walked nearly two months earlier; down to Oare and the Vale of Pewsey beyond. A little green plaque showed that I was again on the Mid-Wilts Way. At first the path was precipitous, and I would have liked to descend really slowly. Apart from anything else, there were interesting butterflies about, blue and brown, and clumps and cushions of intensely blue flowers that I didn't recognise (later research suggested Spring Gentian). But there was now only ten minutes till the bus was due, and I had to go down at a speed that was only possible because of the neatly-formed boot-sized steps; I wondered if they had been cut at some point, or just formed naturally as many walkers negotiated the slope.

I made the bus-stop, opposite the White Hart where I had alighted at the end of March, with three minutes to spare. The bus, of course, was five minutes late, so I could have taken time to look at the butterflies and flowers, but how to know that?

Ten: Oare to Devizes *(20 miles)*

Giant's Grave – Jones's Mill – Butterbur – Croppies – The Man in the Moon – first white elephant – frivolous raven – Roundway Down debacle – Tree Planting Slide – Devizes Wharf – zoological escapism

28th March 2012

I stepped off the bus opposite the White Hart in Oare, and turned down a lane and then onto a footpath in the direction of the tall green hill that was my first objective. At once I was delighted to see a brimstone butterfly, fluttering its wings, the colour of saffron rice, at the spring sun.

A neat wooden board proclaimed this quiet track to be the Oxpath from Maizey to Honeywell, dated 934 – apparently the earliest written record of the village of Oare. Another white sign helped me choose the path towards the hill; then on reaching a strip of woodland the path appeared to turn left, but there was a very clear sign NO FOOTPATH to discourage the rambler from going left, while an ancient stile gave access to a steep earthy slope straight up, under the trees. I followed this route, which none seemed to have trodden recently; fresh shoots of stinging nettles were springing up through the loose earth. At the top edge of the woodland was a barbed wire and webbing fence blocking egress to what was obviously the usual path, ascending the hill from a different starting point. I clambered over the fence, happily without damage to either fence or myself, and tilted my head back to stare up at the summit. It would be a stiff climb to the top of Giant's Grave, some 850 feet high.

At my feet a ladybird crawled, and as I remembered from boyhood, was easily tempted to climb onto a finger. But before I could count the spots it swivelled its red wingcases aside, and flew away. A little further up the hill a red butterfly mounted high on the breeze, and bumble-bees added their drone to the summery impression of cloudless sky and warm sun. I took a zigzag course up the grassy slope to reduce the strain on legs that were out of condition for serious steepness, and reached the summit without expending too much of the energy needed for the rest of the afternoon's walk.

A weatherbeaten post marked this summit as a part of the Mid-Wilts Way. There was a panoramic view in three directions; the defensibility of the site made it attractive in ancient times. There have been finds of late Bronze Age and early Iron Age pottery here,[1] showing that for a while, around three thousand years ago, it was occupied at least intermittently; but it never became a major fort. A mile or less to the east was Martinsell Hill Camp, a large but relatively lightly fortified enclosure that the archaeologists believe was not permanently settled, nor intended to withstand a siege, but could have been used as an occasional assembly point for celebrations or trading, or as an enclosure for stock in hard weather.

[1] Payne et al *op cit*

I wondered who might have been the giant that was buried here, if any. If these hills had been the scene of any battles like Alfred's or Arthur's, it was too long ago for any memory to have survived. But perhaps the earlier era had been more peaceful, the bronze axes used for woodland management rather than slaughtering men. There must have been some stories attached to this hill once.

Long Handle leaned on the great bronze axe, whose handle had earned him his nickname. Of course his mother had not named him that; how would she know that her infant son would grow to be two yards and a span in height, so that the bodger could not take an axe handle out of stock for him, but had to make one to measure? That was a good many years ago now; the one-off handle had lasted well and was darkened yet shiny with age and use. There was still plenty for it to do, but today Long Handle was unaccountably tired, as he gazed out from the hilltop, kept clear of trees by his woodman's labour, harvesting fuel for the potters' kilns nearby.

A stocky figure appeared on the hillside below, climbing doggedly towards the summit. Long Handle sighed inwardly; Furze Twig was not a favourite friend. His gnarled and prickly nature, as rough as his appearance, had given rise to another apt nickname. The clan loved nicknames, a source of endless merriment to all except the one renamed, but Long Handle took care these days not to tease Furze Twig. For a time they had been bitter opponents, and all over the most trivial thing: one ash tree, and whether to fell it, or let it stand yet awhile.

Furze Twig was the older man, a cunning forester; but Long Handle had towered over him, using his physical dominance to carry his point among the other woodmen, and then smugly kept his temper when the small man had exploded. It had been a moment of triumph, and he had savoured it until something woke him the following night. Totally wakeful for no reason he could see, hear, or smell, he stood up and walked quietly out of the hut into the moonlit night.

The moon burned white in a star-strewn sky. Some said she was a goddess, but now Long Handle had a conviction that the moon was a made thing, beautifully made like his axe or its handle. Somebody had made the moon, and the same Somebody had made the whole world, had made him tall and strong, had made Furze Twig small and tough, and had made the ash tree that was in dispute. How did this Somebody see things? How did this Somebody see him? All at once he felt the presence of something so huge that the high moon and the high hill and his tall self seemed tiny in comparison, and words were pressed into his mind, words that he absolutely did not want to hear or contemplate: 'loveless', and 'overbearing', and 'bully'. He wept.

The next day, he apologised to Furze Twig, and the tree was duly felled, to the surprise of the others. But somehow this was not quite right either, it was as if he had only emphasised his magnanimity in condescending to give way, and left the other man with every reason still to feel belittled. And try as he would, he could not love Furze Twig, nor even like him just a bit. He could perhaps stop overbearing and bullying, but how to stop being loveless?

And now, here came the prickly little fellow again. How to love him? What sacrifice would be enough for the crime of not loving? There were words in his mind again, quiet words without the overwhelming sense of hugeness of that moonlit night. 'I will love Furze Twig for you. And I am the sacrifice.' The view to the east suddenly became hazy, his long legs buckled, and Long Handle found himself lying on the hilltop, looking up at the sky, then at the puzzled, wrinkled face of Furze Twig, as the latter bent over him, and reached out a hand. But his left hand, which was uppermost, would not move, nor could he speak.

Long Handle realised what was happening; he had seen his grandfather die in this way. He rolled a little, raised his right hand, pointed to himself, then made digging motions with his palm, then patted the turf beside him. He was glad that the other did not argue, or tell him that he would recover, but simply nodded dumbly, as if he too had lost the power of speech. Finally, with a great effort, he raised the bronze axe head and pressed it into Furze Twig's grasp. He saw tears start in the little man's eyes, then a most uncharacteristic grin as, hefting the axe, Furze Twig showed him with the edge of his hand how he would have to cut more than a foot off the handle to use it. Long Handle returned the smile with half of his face.

'My unfriend weeps for me, and forgives me,' he thought in wonderment, as the blue sky faded from sight.

Probably no-one was buried here at all, and the shape of the hill alone had earned Giant's Grave its name. At my feet were little blue flowers that at first glance I took to be selfheal, but which turned out to be ground ivy. This used to be known as Alehoof, for it was used in the brewing of beer before hops arrived in England from the continent. Culpeper lists other names: Haymaids, Turnhoof, Gill-go-by-ground, and Catsfoot, from the shape of the leaf. He observes that it clarifies cloudy liquids, which explains its use for ale, but also that it has many medical uses, promoting the healing of wounds and lesions: 'the juice of it boiled with a little honey and verdigrease, doth wonderfully cleanse fistulas... and stays the spreading or eating of cancers and ulcers.'[1]

On the hilltop were also many flat spreading rosettes of thistles, and the grey leaves of silverweed. I decided not to make the detour to Martinsell Hill Camp; my reading had suggested there would not be a lot to see there. Instead I turned down a deep hollow way, warm and sunlit through the branches of the trees that grew above. Another Brimstone fluttered ahead of me, and celandines and primroses continued the yellow spring theme, counterbalanced by more purple-blue ground ivy. Some way down the slope, the sunken path crossed another in a wide dell, and I left the Mid-Wilts Way to take the shortest route down to the canal. The path was well-trodden and notably dry, baked and cracked and bleached by the sun and the lack of rain in an unusually dry winter.

[1] Culpeper, *op cit*

An orange-tip butterfly was conspicuous against the hedge. Eventually the dry footpath became a quiet tree-lined lane. The canal was not far away; it was good to descend from the lane and be walking beside water again, the wide arch of Milkhouse Water Bridge and a moored broad-beamed barge both witnessing to the Kennet & Avon's fourteen-foot gauge. Charles Sorley loved to walk along this peaceful waterway: 'In the winter the downs, in the summer the forest, but the Kennet & Avon canal …in spring is worth ten of these.'[1]

The two-note song of a chiff-chaff echoed along the water, under tall trees, and for once I was able to see the bird, rather than just hearing it. I watched it flitting from perch to perch in a goat willow, its song accompanied by the drone of many bumble-bees that were investigating the fat catkins. Another small bird flew across the canal, its slaty blue and pale pink plumage and black eye-stripe proclaiming its nuthatch identity. A second nuthatch joined it, in what looked like early nesting activity. And as I turned to walk on, a wren flipped up from the water's edge, across the towpath right in front of my knees, and sang to me from the tangled undergrowth two feet away.

Next to a moored narrowboat, three weatherbeaten characters sprawled in folding chairs on the towpath; as I approached, the huge shaggy Alsatian with them moved eagerly in my direction, happy to make a new friend.

'She's alright – a real softie.'

'She'll lick you to death.'

This was only a small exaggeration; my forearms were distinctly damp for a while.

Sooner than expected, I came to the north-east entrance to Jones's Mill, a wildlife reserve I'd been planning to visit, and was at first disappointed that it appeared to be a field much like any other. But as I ventured further in, it began to show signs of marshiness, even in this exceptionally dry period, and the path through the lower field was provided with duckboards, raised well above the level of the boggy meadow, which was sprinkled with the bright yellow of marsh marigolds. I saw enough to realise how much more interesting and attractive it would be in a month's time.

Further in, the path led under tangled trees amid winding watercourses, a scene that was less shaded than it would be once the trees were in leaf. Information boards had promised dragonflies, and these streams and pools were classic dragonfly habitat, but there were none to be seen in late March, even when it was as warm as this. Still, the intricate pathways through the wetland made very pleasant walking, as did the open meadow beyond, through which two young women were walking six energetic little terriers. A path at the far end of the reserve led back up to the canal.

[1] Sorley, CH (ed Sorley, WR, 1919) *The Letters of Charles Sorley* CUP

Progressing westward again on the towpath, I was beginning to look forward to the French Horn, a hostelry at Pewsey Wharf recommended by a number of authorities. The afternoon was absurdly warm for the time of year, and my water-bottle was empty. Sadly, the French Horn adhered to opening hours from the bad old days: it had been open until three, and would open again at six, but at ten past four on a hot thirsty afternoon, the wayfarer was faced with a shut door. Pressing on for three miles, risking dehydration, did not seem as sensible an option as walking half a mile into Pewsey, even though that would add a mile to my day's journey.

The walk in and back, along a busy main road, was not much fun, but the refreshment at the Royal Oak, consisting of Henry's IPA, was very welcome; the innsign actually offering a 'Welcome to Wadworthshire'. Returning to the canal, I was glad to be on my way again, somewhat later than intended, but it still seemed probable that I would arrive well within the daylight available.

All around a bend in the canal were flower spikes of something I didn't quite recognise, something vaguely orchid-like, pale pinky-creamy coned clusters of flowers sticking straight up out of the grass. Later research suggested Toothwort, *lathrea squamaria*, which flowers in March and is noted as growing along the Kennet & Avon. Toothwort is a parasite, growing on the roots of hazel or elm, which seemed plausible here. However, Toothwort has one-sided flower spikes, and these were clearly all-sided. In shape they were more like Broomrape, the many varieties of which flower considerably later. Broomrape, too, is parasitic on the roots of trees or other plants.

An inquiry to the Wiltshire Wildlife Trust, to clarify the plant's identity, proved my ignorance; it was Butterbur, *petasites hybridus,* and reading up about this lover of canals and streamsides, I realised that I had seen it a number of times before on the Four Points Ramble: in Barrowford, Lancashire, and on the northern Oxford Canal in Warwickshire. Culpeper notes that the flowers appear early, in February and March, and the leaves later; and judges that it is 'under the dominion of the Sun, and therefore is a great strengthener of the heart, and clearer of the vital spirit.'[1]

As I followed the Kennet & Avon westwards, the sun was low enough to shine up off the water as well as down from just above the tree-tops, the combined dazzle making it difficult to appreciate the beauty of the scenery, unless I paused and turned, to look back at the stretch I had just walked. Eventually I reached Wilcot Wide Water, where the canal broadened into a long lake, fringed with reeds and trees, and embellished with a most elegant bridge at the far end. There was a heavy splash under the bank almost at my feet, and a swirl of water that suggested something quite big – otter? Pike? But nothing was visible, apart from the heron on the far side of the wide, flying majestically eastwards above the trees.

[1] Culpeper, *op cit*

The wide, and the bridge, were constructed to appease the local Lady of the Manor, who objected to a canal through her land unless it was designed to look like a parkland feature, rather than a workaday commercial canal. She got her way; the bridge was built of smoother, finer stone than the average rough and rustic structure, adorned with balusters and much carved detail, and unofficially dubbed Ladies Bridge.

Beyond Ladies Bridge was a very welcome bench, where it was pleasant to take five minutes in the evening sun, contemplating the row of narrowboats on the opposite bank: *Jenny Wren*, *Isle of Avalon*, *Cerdic*, and *Stargazer*. West of here the canal was wide open, with no hedges to divide it from the broad fields on either side.

The odd sharp peak of Picked Hill rose up close by on the right, as I followed the towpath and wondered where the next bridge was. Huge mushroom-shaped growths of Tussock Sedge lined the near edge of the water. Finally I came to a bridge where the towpath crossed to the south bank, proving that this was indeed Woodborough Fields Bridge.

Coming round the bend beyond the bridge, I caught sight of the Alton Barnes White Horse on the hillside, bright in the low sunlight, a welcome sign that journey's end for the day was near. The horse is in no way prehistoric, having been cut in 1812, 'a poor specimen of a white horse' Hippisley Cox calls it,[1] and indeed it showed little of the grace or elegance or dynamic energy of some of the thirteen or more other white horses that adorn every second hillside in Wiltshire.

The field path that made a short cut to Well Cottage B&B was easy to find, and soon I was stretching my limbs and soaking up a large pot of tea, recovering energy before heading out in the last of the light to see what food the Barge Inn at Honey Street Wharf had to offer.

Honey Street Wharf had once been a hive of industry: canal carriers Robbins, Lane & Pinnegar with their own fleet of barges; a boatyard that built craft for the River Wey, the River Avon, and the Basingstoke Canal; and a timber yard. The Barge Inn was once a slaughterhouse and bakehouse as well as brewing its own beer. Most of this trade had been slowly strangled by the neglect of the canal in the twentieth century, finally dying in the 1940s; but there was still a timber yard giving off a fragrance of sawn softwood in the twilight.

The Barge lived up to its many recommendations (though the booklet I had that named it as a Courage house was clearly rather out of date), and I was happy to refuel on a magnificent curried lamb shank, and some locally brewed Croppie ale. I wondered if it had been brewed on the premises, since the pump plaque named the brewer as Honeystreet Ales, but the bartender, offering taster thimblefuls of all three ales on offer, said no, nearby, but not actually in the building. The greenish liquid that went by the name of Alien Abduction was certainly a unique experience, but I would not have wanted a whole pint of it, and I settled for what I would have selected on grounds of lowest alcohol, even if I hadn't been offered the taster. Croppie, at 4%, was just as its website describes it, a 'golden ale with a satisfying aftertaste'.

[1] Hippisley Cox, *op cit*

Bright stars, shining planets, and a crescent moon, lit my way back to the cottage.

The Man in the Moon

29th March 2012

Breakfast in the conservatory, looking out on a spacious well-kept garden, gave the opportunity to see a dunnock perch on a stone wall alongside the blue flowers. Waiting for the bacon and eggs, I glanced at a tourist leaflet for the Pewsey area, and was struck by the picture of a Roman gold pin, topped with two lovebirds and inscribed LUCIANUS, that had been found here in Woodborough. So well-to-do Romans also found the Vale of Pewsey a pleasant place to live.

The climb from the valley up into the hills was less stiff than I'd feared; I was entertained along the way by a group of rooks poking around in a field of stubble, strutting here and there with a most self-important air, one of them catching my eye as if to say 'who are you looking at?'

The path slanted up on a broad grassy shelf on the shoulder of Walker's Hill; though I didn't realise it at the time, I was probably treading again in the footsteps of travellers over thousands of years, for this is thought to have been the main route for long-distance Ridgeway travellers, the link between Avebury Down and Salisbury Plain. Well Cottage, where I had slept and breakfasted, also lay on this Great Ridgeway route.[1]

From Walker's Hill all the way to the far side of Roundway Down, there was hardly a moment when one or more skylarks were not singing; the sound seemed natural to the high grassy places. The sound must have been equally familiar to the clerical poet George Herbert, rector of a little rural parish further south in Wiltshire. For him it was an image in sound of the Christian believers' praise for their Redeemer:

Lord, who createdst man in wealth and store,
Though foolishly he lost the same,
Decaying more and more,
Till he became
Most poor:
With thee
O let me rise
As larks, harmoniously,
And sing this day thy victories:
Then shall the fall further the flight in me.

[1] Timperley, HW & Brill, E (1965) *Ancient Trackways of Wessex* Phoenix House

Apart from the many skylarks, I noticed a few yellowhammers, one with the yellowest head I'd ever seen, pure plain yellow without any streaks of brown, and almost as bright as the flowers on the gorse he was perching on. He was close enough for a photograph, and posed patiently until just one second before I was ready. Shrugging off the tiny disappointment, I wandered a little uncertainly onwards through the Pewsey Downs nature reserve, and on a long loop round the high shoulder of Milk Hill, finding myself once more on the Mid-Wilts Way, before coming to the route I was aiming for, the Wansdyke.

It stretched away west and east, a tall rampart with a deep ditch on its north side; from the bottom of the ditch the rampart loomed twenty or thirty feet high in places. The Wansdyke is an impressive structure clearly intended to defend against, or deter, an enemy to the north. Who built it is still a matter for speculation, for there is little direct evidence and no clear consensus among the experts. The name 'Wansdyke' is presumed to be a contraction of 'Woden's Dyke', a name given by the Saxons that suggests it was already here when they arrived in the fifth century. If they had built so impressive a structure from scratch, surely the name of the king that ordered it to be built would have been commemorated, as in Offa's case. There has been a suggestion that the Wansdyke could have been a British defence against Ceawlin's advance from the Thames valley in the 570s,[1] but it seems curious to build so imposing a defence against the north when Saxons were also advancing in the south. It makes more sense to guess that the British leader at the time simply improved an existing defensive line.

However, Pitt-Rivers had already noted in the 19th century that the line of Wansdyke followed a Roman Road for some way, and his excavations found no pre-Roman or early Roman material, so narrowing the most likely date of construction to between the third and early sixth centuries, though historians were puzzled as to the scenario that would have justified such a massive undertaking. Having said that, our modern age offers plenty of examples of huge capital projects that turned out to be a waste of effort almost as soon as they were finished. Perhaps the Wansdyke was the first white elephant, an order that could not be withdrawn because of the loss of face that half-completion would have caused.

Described by Major and Burrow as 'seven miles of unparalleled loneliness',[2] this magnificent earthwork was exhilarating to walk, rolling over the hills so that from each vantage point you could see the next couple of miles and be confident that you would not lose your way. Once or twice a red butterfly scudded away on the wind, too distant to identify, but most probably a Peacock. At one point I encountered four impressively horned sheep, creamy wool flecked with light brown, and dark grey horns turning under and forwards. Later I tried to identify them from the photo I'd taken, but no breed seemed to match their description; perhaps they were crossbreeds. Later still, I discovered they were probably Jacob's Sheep.

[1] Cunliffe, 1993 *op cit*

[2] Major, JF & Burrow, EJ (1926) *The Mystery of Wansdyke*

Coming over the shoulder of Tan Hill, I passed the highest point of the entire course of the Wansdyke, meticulously noted by Major and Burrow as 903 feet. Away to the north was the green cone of that most mysterious structure, Silbury Hill, whose origin and function still divides academic opinion. As a sundial it seems a little over-engineered. Ahead, the Wansdyke ran down again, before gradually rising to Morgan's Hill in the distance. Here and there, on the rampart and in the ditch, were the 'storm-stunted hawthorn bushes, gnarled and aged' that Richard Jefferies describes as characteristic of these ancient down-land routes. The numerous blue flowers of ground ivy were signs of spring; but some stunted ash trees still bore the dull brown dried keys from the previous autumn, with no sign of this year's leaves emerging from their black buds.

Beyond a little strip of woodland I encountered more sheep I couldn't identify: handsome beasts with brown wool, white faces, and no horns. Here the Wansdyke path, which had hitherto mostly followed the crest of the rampart, switched to the lip on the north side of the ditch, as the dyke curved round a steep hillside towards Morgan's Hill, now quite close. A kestrel took off nearby and skimmed over the valley into the north wind.

Richard Jefferies observed the way a kestrel uses the wind: 'As the breeze strikes him aslant his course he seems to fly for a short time partly on one side, like a skater sliding on the outer edge.'[1] It is an odd coincidence that, writing in the same decade, the poet Hopkins was inspired to use the same simile to describe the same bird: 'as a skate's heel sweeps smooth on a bow-bend' – and yet there is no possibility that either writer had read the other before he wrote.

It was a little unusual to see two crows and a raven perched together on the fence along the top of the Wansdyke; the difference in size was very noticeable when they were so close to each other. As I approached, all took off, and another raven joined them. The first raven performed a quick victory roll right under the beak of the nearest crow, which seemed not to have noticed; the raven pair then soared over the updraught at the edge of the hill, and one continued his jinking and tumbling, enjoying his mastery of the air. The crows drifted away in the other direction.

[1] Jefferies, 1879 *op cit*

Dear Mr Four Points Rambler,

We are saddened to find that you have so far taken leave of your critical judgment as to be impressed by the aerial frivolity of a raven suffering a temporary loss of dignity.

We prefer not to react in any way to such aerobatic nonsense, as we do not wish to encourage undue levity. You too would do well to refrain from applauding such abuse of the glorious providence of flight.

Yours sincerely, Primula Crowe

I doubt if I shall ever meet a crow that does not disapprove of me.

The area of rough moorland grass at the brow of Morgan's Hill is a Wiltshire Wildlife Trust nature reserve, and noted for its butterflies in spring, but I was either too early in the year, or the wind was a little too strong and too chilly, for any butterflies to be on the wing. I paused to enjoy the broad view northwards, the little church of Calstone Wellington prominent at the foot of the steep slope, before turning to follow a bridleway across a golf course, keeping an eye open for stray flying golfballs as I descended the slope. It was a fine setting for a course, with extensive views south over Roundway Down. I followed a track southwards, then a lane westwards, to have a good look at this historic battlefield. From the name, and a very cursory glance at the map, I had imagined Roundway Down to be a typical broad, slightly convex plateau; in fact it was slightly concave, shaped like a bowl, or even more like a broad rectangular platter. The high plain was enclosed by long low hills: Morgan's Hill to the NE, behind me; King's Play Hill to the NW, on my right; and Roundway Hill to the SE, on my left. Only straight ahead was there no rising ground, which explained how the battle had unfolded.

On the 13th July, 1643, the Royalists were besieged in Devizes, but a force of cavalry was approaching from the north to attempt to raise the siege. The Parliamentarian forces ranged themselves here to hinder that approach, infantry in the centre, cavalry on the flanks, as was conventional practice. The Royalist horse then charged both flanks, ignoring the centre, and soon put their opponents to flight. The shape of Roundway Down, and the direction of attack, caused the defeated Parliamentarian cavalry to flee south-westwards, where they suddenly found themselves facing an abrupt drop of 300 feet, over which they were forced headlong. The bottom of this precipice became a pile of dead and dying horses and men, and the stream was thereafter known as the 'Bloody Ditch'.

Meanwhile the Parliamentarian infantry were still standing on Roundway Down, bemused at having no opposing infantry to attack or defend themselves against. After a while, the Royalist troops that had been shut in Devizes came up, and together with the victorious cavalry, completed one of the major Royalist victories of the Civil War.[1]

[1] Burne, AH (2002) *The Battlefields of England* Penguin

I followed the woodland path round on the high contour, aware of the steepness of the slope on my right. All this woodland had grown up since the seventeenth century, and this would then have been an open slope, down which some of the fleeing Parliamentarians would have plunged, though the bulk of them went down the even steeper slope further north, on the other side of Oliver's Camp. At one point the path emerged onto a little open space on the shoulder of the hill, where there was a bench that I was glad to sit on for five minutes and contemplate the view of Oliver's Camp, a curious grassy platform halfway up the nearby promontory, which had once been fortified, but according to the archaeologists, never occupied. Admirably defended as it was from an enemy below, it was very exposed to attack from above, and had perhaps only proved useful as a little level and sheltered space to grow a crop.

The path eventually left the woodland, and rejoined a lane before another path traced a straight dry line down towards the town of Devizes. Below the steepest slope, someone had recently planted lines of native trees, ash and thorn and hazel, on either side of the path, and new green leaves were just breaking out to show that most of the planting had been successful. I wondered whether the trees I had helped plant a couple of months before, away up on the Welsh border, were similarly showing signs of new life. I had had a new tune running through my head that day, as I inserted alder and ash saplings:

Tree Planting Slide

A long avenue of tall mature trees led in towards Devizes; at first the town seemed to be getting no nearer, then all of a sudden the canal was right in front of me. I had been imagining a canalside pub for a late lunch, but there didn't appear to be one, though the Crown was not far away and still open and ready to serve a roll and soup – excellent leek and potato – and more of Henry's IPA. The barman put my purchases on a tab, which I'm not particularly used to, and half an hour after I'd left the pub and was wandering round the town appreciating the varied architecture, I was mortified to realise I'd walked out without paying. Hurrying back, I paid up and advised the barman (who hadn't even noticed I'd gone) not to use tabs for wrinkly citizens with colander memories. From the Crown I strolled back to the Wharf, where so much of the freight had been loaded and unloaded, in the early days of the Kennet & Avon, 'the great channel', wrote William Cobbett in 1830, 'through which the produce of the country is carried away to be devoured by the idlers, the thieves, and the prostitutes, who are *all* tax-eaters, in the WENS of Bath and London.'[1]

[1] Cobbett, W (1830) *Rural Rides*

Cobbett gave a one-sided view of the traffic; much useful material also arrived in Devizes: coal, ashes, stone, flints, salt, bricks and timber, to balance the departing corn, flour, and cheese. However, once the railway was opened in 1841, the bulk of this traffic disappeared.[1]

Much later, this wharf became the starting-point for the Devizes to Westminster Canoe Race; a feat of endurance involving the negotiation of 76 locks in 125 miles, which settled into something like its present form in 1949, having grown out of a number of individual challenges and wagers in earlier years. It is always held at Easter, which may expose competitors to the full variety of English weather: individuals have been treated for both heatstroke and frostbite in different years.[2] The popularity of this event, which has attracted much interest and many entries from the military and from uniformed youth organisations over the years, helped to raise awareness of the Kennet & Avon and sustain interest in its restoration during the long wait for the canal to re-open. The petition to save the canal from abandonment was also taken to Westminster by canoe in 1956.

From the wharf I resumed the amble round the town centre that had been interrupted by remembering my unpaid bill. I was impressed by the fine 15th-century tower of St Mary the Virgin, but saddened to see the church no longer used for worship, and closed to casual visitors, so there was no chance to see the interior, parts of which date back to Norman times. It appears, however, that there are far-reaching plans for future use of the building; and the parish of St John with St Mary is thriving, concentrating services at St John's.

In the Market Square was an intriguing statue above a doorway: a stocky figure with a heavy log as a staff, and a fat python-like snake curled round it. He turned out to be Aesculapius, god of medicine; the house had been home to a surgeon in the early nineteenth century.

Later on, half-sitting only semi-comfortably on the stainless steel tubes that passed for seating in the bus shelter, waiting for a much-delayed afternoon bus, I was struck by how zoological were the pub names in the Market Square. The Pelican faced the Black Swan, and their brightly-painted innsigns were flanked by the Bear and the Dolphin, all commemorating exotic species that were unlikely to be manifest in the flesh in Devizes in the foreseeable future: romantic escapism in workaday Wiltshire.

[1] Kennet DC (1977) 'The History of Devizes Wharf', *The Butty* No **75**
[2] Crosley, GH (1976) 'The Devizes to Westminster Canoe Race', *The Butty* No **71**

Eleven: Devizes to Lacock *(9 miles)*

Devizes – dangerous heresy – sanctuary for Hubert – delayed start – Three around Three – slow going – Lacock – child bride and royal bastard – Ne Sai Que Je Die

13th April 2012

A week after Easter, in between my arrival in Devizes on foot, and resuming the walk from there two months later, I passed through with Ishbel, to take a leisurely look round. She was quite surprised that Devizes was the name of a town, having only come across the word in her native Scotland as the name of a metrical psalm tune. In fact it proved difficult to locate in the Scottish Psalter, only appearing in odd references on the internet, not strongly associated with any one psalm, but fitting neatly with a couple of related Scriptural Paraphrases:

His sacred blood hath washed our souls
From sin's polluted stain;
His stripes have healed us, and his death
Revived our souls again.

We all, like sheep, had gone astray
In ruin's fatal road:
On him were our transgressions laid;
He bore the mighty load.
(Isaiah 53:7/8)

No hope can on the law be built
Of justifying grace;
The law, that shows the sinner's guilt,
Condemns him to his face.

Jesus! How glorious is thy grace!
When in thy name we trust,
Our faith receives a righteousness
That makes the sinner just.
(Romans 3:22/3)

Devizes

The last line of each verse is repeated to the last three and a half bars of the music. The references, in both Old and New Testaments, confirm that salvation comes through God's actions, rather than our own good deeds or the offices of the Church. Here in Devizes there were some that were clear about this even in the Middle Ages, though the ecclesiastical authorities tried to eradicate views that challenged their version of Christianity. In 1434, a hundred years before the Reformation in England, William Wakeham of Devizes was forced to abjure his 'denial of transubstantiation and the power of the priest, opposition to pilgrimages and to the worship of crosses and images', and was accused of taking part in Bible study. Three years later he was judged to have relapsed into his Lollard practices and opinions, reported as believing the true church to be the people, rather than the building, which was merely stone and wood.[1]

[1] Thomson, *op cit*

All of this would make William Wakeham an unremarkable Evangelical today, but at the time he was marked down as a dangerous heretic.

Devizes used to be known as 'the Vies', from the Latin *ad divisas*, 'at the boundaries'; Leland wrote that it 'standithe on a ground sumwhat clyvinge, and most occupied by clothiers. The beawty of it is all in one strete'.[1] The one street he referred to was presumably the Market Place, running on via the High Street to Long Street; and if you consider the buildings between St John's Street and the High Street as an island in one broad route, then much of interest today is still in this one street. We photographed a number of handsome buildings: the Corn Exchange, the Bear Hotel, and the Market Cross, and then found our way to a pleasant teashop in St John's Street for morning coffee, before visiting the headquarters of the Wiltshire Wildlife Trust, one of the beneficiary charities of this book. I had thought of touring Wadworth's brewery, until we saw the cost of a tour, and contented ourselves with a quick browse in the visitor centre. There was no time to look at the remains of Devizes Castle, mentioned by Leland as one of the sights of the town:

> Ther is a castell on the south west side of the towne stately avauncyd apon an highe ground, defendyd partly by nature, and partly withe dykes the yere where of is cast up a slope, and that of a greate height to defence of the waulle.
>
> This castle was made in Henry the first days by one Rogar Bysshope of Salisbyrye, Chaunselar and Treaswrar to the Kynge. Suche a pece of castle worke so costly and strongly was never afore nor sence set up by any bysshope of England.[2]

In 1233 this stronghold was used to imprison Hubert de Burgh, Earl of Kent, the last Justiciar of England, who had been the most powerful man in the land during Henry III's minority. However he had also made enemies at this time, and the Bishop of Winchester finally had him arrested on serious charges. The watch over him in Devizes Castle must have been slack, and de Burgh would have noticed its weaknesses. The septuagenarian was experienced in such matters, having been imprisoned before, in France, and having also been a jailer himself, responsible for keeping Arthur of Brittany in custody. The story goes that on Michaelmas Eve, one of his servants carried Hubert on his back all through the castle and out of the great gate, and from there to St John's church, where he claimed sanctuary.

[1] Smith, *op cit*
[2] Smith, *op cit*

When his captors realised where de Burgh was, their shock and embarrassment led them to violate the laws of Sanctuary, entering the church and dragging the earl back to the castle. The bishop of Salisbury reacted strongly, excommunicating the sanctuary-breakers, and ordering the captive to be restored to the church, from where his supporters later rescued him. In the end a reconciliation was negotiated, and de Burgh's name cleared.

22nd May 2012

I alighted from the bus at the same stop in Devizes Market Square where I'd waited two months before. I'd intended to get here by twelve noon, which would have been quite late enough to start a day's walk, but 20 minutes' lateness of one train led to a missed connection, which led to another missed connection, which led to getting caught up in Olympic Torch disruption, which resulted in missing yet another bus, and so now it was 2 o'clock, which meant that much of my planned walk could not be completed, due to the need to find a bus to get home again. Therefore I would not be able to complete the last sections of Book 6 that week, which meant that I would need to come south again at a later date. So First Great Western's 20 minutes lateness would in the end cost me at least two days.

I wondered in what way this might be providential; meanwhile it illustrated the pompous folly of politicians pledging untold billions to high-speed rail projects. In all the unnumbered times I'd been disappointed and let down by public transport, it had never been because the trains were not fast enough. Before we need trains that are faster, we need trains that are more punctual, more reliable, more frequent, and above all, trains that go to more places – all the places that Dr Beeching stopped them from going. More carriages, more seats, more luggage space, and more legroom would all be more helpful than greater speed.

Anyway, it was too nice a day to be really cross; I should have known better than to expect a trouble-free journey, and so I set off, past the towering brick pile of Wadworth's brewery, and joined the canal towpath at the Town Bridge. The first few hundred yards, alongside the upper locks of the Caen Hill flight, but before the steepest part of the incline, were clearly popular with local strollers: girls in high heels pushing prams and buggies, pensioners with dogs and without dogs, drinkers with cans in hand; everyone here was enjoying the Kennet & Avon.

Having passed five locks, still anticipating the really steep bit, I finally came to the expected view, which I'd seen in a hundred photographs but never before in reality: the dizzy perspective of dozens of balance-beams ranged one behind the other down the hill, long side-pounds stretching away northwards. Here at the top was a little café, run by the K&A Canal Trust, that seemed to be the destination for quite a few of the strollers on this warm day. I bought a cold drink and got my water bottle refilled, and was very grateful for the café being just where it was.

As I passed the next lock, a couple of lads enjoying a beer called out 'How far have you come?'

I hesitated, vacillating between 514 miles on the Four Points Ramble from Arnside, or sixty-odd miles from Taunton that day, or barely a mile on the day's walk so far; in the end I said weakly, 'not far', aware again that under the surface I was still quite upset that the day's original plan was unachievable.

The steepest fifteen or so locks of the flight were soon past; downhill was easy going, and I was able to look back up at the familiar sight of the serried rows of black balance-beams and white footbridges, as the canal rose eastward up the hill. For decades this magnificent feat of engineering was unnavigable; the last working boat locked up the flight in 1948, and Caen Hill Locks were not officially re-opened until 1990. In the 1970s, a passing long-distance walker found the locks 'derelict', and was sceptical as to any successful restoration: 'I think it will be many a long day before a boat "locks up" there'.[1]

There were still a few more locks before Foxhangers; next to one pound I was distracted by the rasping song of a bird in the reeds. It was astonishingly loud and quite distinctive, and briefly I caught a glimpse of a little brown bird. When I reached for the camera, however, what flew up and posed with the utmost cuteness, clasping a slender reed stem, was a blue tit. I felt reasonably sure that I had not been listening to a blue tit; we have blue tits in our back garden, and they don't sound like that at all. An elderly couple came by, and the man said, 'Is that the reed warblers again?' I said I didn't know; but it seemed that was what the song had been. A later listen to recordings confirmed the identification.

Nearby, across the canal, stood a most desirable residence, solid and square and probably Georgian, with a separate double garage with extension and dormers, and a wharf arm accommodating a smart green and red narrowboat. If these fortunate folk ever felt the need to downsize and move somewhere less quiet, perhaps they would consider a house swap?

Beyond Foxhangers was Caen Hill Marina, a new development with its own lift bridge across the entrance; and opposite that, a symphony in white on green, a great swathe of may blossom and pussy willow above cow parsley, hogweed, and comfrey, all sporting white flowers in great abundance. Further on was vetch in several shades from blood-red to lilac; the brown spikes of last year's purple loosestrife still standing; and at the water's edge, the vivid light green of Hemlock Water Dropwort, *oenanthe crocata*, one of the deadliest things in English nature. The roots, apparently, look rather like parsnip, but will kill you in hours if you try eating them.

[1] Crisp, BW (1976) 'The towpath is for walking' *The Butty* No **72**

I was certainly ready to eat something; it was gone three o'clock and a very long time since breakfast. Behind Sells Green Bridge was a smart red board, contrasting fetchingly with the green and white of tall grasses and cow parsley, and advertising 'good food' at the Three Magpies, very precisely located 281 yards away. I walked 281 yards with alacrity, passing a Caravanners' Club site on the way and wondering if our friend Barbara had ever stayed there. She was part of a circle of friends that combined caravan ownership with folk musicianship; so perhaps this site was used to hearing ceilidh music on summer evenings.

Three Around Three

G D G C G C D G D G C G D7 G

G C G D G C C D G

The Three Magpies was open, offering some very welcome Henry's IPA, but nothing more than crisps and nuts to eat at this late hour, well after three. It wasn't 'good food' as I would understand the words, but it was at least enough to stave off starvation, and as I relaxed in the cool of the bar, I realised how hot it had become outside, and was not totally dismayed to be going no further. 'The destination of a Ramble,' as Mike Harding says, 'is often moveable.'[1] There was time enough to go on, but not to get as far as any sensible point to start the next day's walk, so I took my time over the beer and nuts, and re-planned the next excursion.

A stroll along and across the canal, and up the hill to Seend, gave the opportunity to cool off further in a medieval church, before catching the bus to Trowbridge.

24th May 2012

For this day's walk I had no intention of letting public transport fail to deliver me to the start on time, and instead persuaded my sister to drop me at my start point. She had not yet visited Lacock Abbey, whereas I had, so she could go round the building and grounds, while I walked the five miles from Sells Green. Punctually at eleven, Madge dropped me at the Three Magpies; the journey from Taunton had taken an hour and forty minutes, compared to Tuesday's scheduled two hours forty minutes, which the cumulative delays had turned into four hours forty minutes. Small wonder that it is so difficult to persuade England's motorists not to use their cars.

I took a pleasant meadow path westwards, before turning right and under the old Devizes – Holt branch line, here appearing as the bridge abutments where the footpath had once run under an embankment. The Devizes line was only a minor branch, but linked at both ends to main lines, so that on occasion it could be used as part of an alternative line from Bristol to London, if one of the main lines was blocked.

[1] Harding, *op cit*

Beyond the old railway was a field of waist-high grass; the path was well-waymarked, but appeared to have been little used. One or two people had come this way recently, but no more than that, and the path was only visible as a darker line through the waving grass. At feet and ankles level, the remains of a heavy dew was soakingly evident. Crossing the next road, signposts confirmed that this was still the right of way, but underfoot there was less to show that I was following the right route. Coming to the corner of one field, no way out at all was visible, which is always worrying; then suddenly a gap appeared, and a stile that led to a succession of broad green lanes, making very pleasant walking. There was abundant comfrey, its drooping flowers appearing here in white, there in purple; and the broad fretty leaves of hemlock were a common feature of the hedges.

I turned left onto a farm track, still reasonably confident I was following a bridleway marked on the map, though there were no signposts or waymarkers. A hare bounded across the track, and disappeared into long grass; and a couple of boldly coloured cock pheasants paced slowly on the edge of a field. Following the track as it led roughly north-eastwards, it became increasingly hard to relate it to what was on the map. Two parallel lines of pylons, and various copses and spinneys and strips of woodland, all corresponded exactly to the map, meaning I could identify my position precisely; but the farm track was not at the same angle as the bridleway on the map, nor was the junction of bridleways, directly under one of the lines of pylons according to the map, anywhere to be seen in reality.

I had perforce to take a rough line towards the identifiable point on the skyline where woodland met lane, and the bridleway supposedly emerged; but growing crops meant that I had to go round two edges of each field, rather than diagonally across, as the bridleway was marked. Underfoot was fairly hard going, either baked clay ridged by tractor tyre treads, or soft mud where the remains of rain several days before still lingered. I was beginning to wonder if I had been over-optimistic in predicting my arrival time in Lacock; so far I'd barely covered two miles of the route in the first hour, though I'd walked a fair bit further than that. A fat grey partridge distracted me from such worries, whirring away from the other side of a field.

Coming up to the road at Sandridge, there seemed at first no sign of an exit to the field, but at the last moment a narrow overgrown gap appeared, and at the roadside was a signpost that showed that as far as Wiltshire County Council were concerned, this was where the bridleway emerged.

From here to Lacock was at least downhill, and I hoped I would be able to regain lost time. 'A Ramble,' according to Mike Harding, 'is a gentle meandering sort of walk in the countryside';[1] as so often, this wasn't quite turning out like that. If it had been less meandering, it could perhaps have been gentler.

Sandridge was a charming little hamlet; I was impressed by the amount of vetch flowering on one roadside bank, and noticed also the yellow flowers of sow thistle and wild radish. A tiny brick building looked like a former wayside chapel, though now converted to a dwelling. The beginning of the next footpath was clearly marked, next to a wood full of white ramsons; but further down the hill the problems began. The map marked two paths as diverging, but there was nothing on the ground to show exactly where either of them ran.

At one point I had to decide whether to walk to the left or the right of a hedge and ditch; left looked likelier, but when I'd waded my way through long grass for some two hundred yards, I saw over the hedge a tiny waymarker that showed I should have made the other choice. The hedge and ditch were not surmountable, and I had to retrace my steps, trying to remember that I liked walking through the countryside, and that the smell of new-mown hay was very pleasant, not to mention the sight of brimstone and orange-tip butterflies, which contrast so delightfully with fresh green foliage, so an extra quarter-mile should be a bonus, not an irritation. North Wiltshire was described by Cobbett as 'a rather flat, enclosed country [with] …a bottom of marl, clay, or flat stone… a country for cattle, fat sheep, cheese, and bacon',[2] and this rich country was certainly enjoyable to stroll through, if one wasn't in too much of a hurry.

At least I now knew I was on the right path, and it proved easy enough to follow, though little-trodden and not quick going through the long grass, thenceforward to Hack Farm. From here was roadwalking for a mile or so, and I was able to stride out to regain time, startled and pleased by the sudden flight across the road of a Greater Spotted woodpecker, red markings flashing in the black-and-white.

I was looking out for the point where I could leave the road and follow a meadow path to Lacock that would also trace a little of the route of the old Wilts & Berks Canal. The beginning of the path, like all the paths I'd walked so far, was clearly marked where it left the road; but in the meadow there was no sign of the path underfoot. I decided that since I was already late, the chance of losing more time by going astray was not one I should take, and so I returned to the road to make the best time possible to Lacock.

[1] Harding, *op cit*
[2] Cobbett, *op cit*

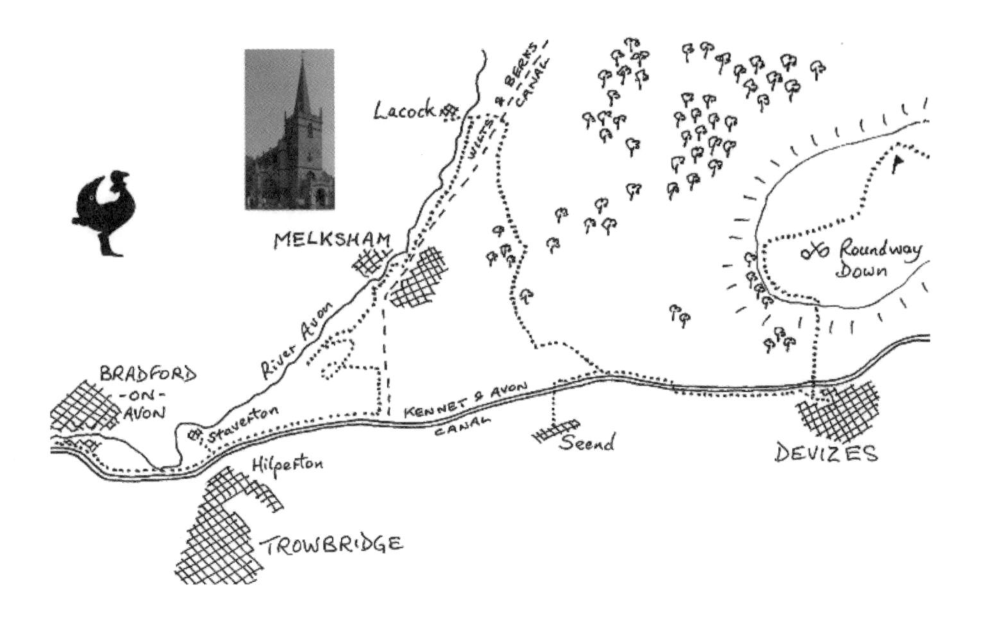

Map for chapters 10 -12

In Bewley Common I passed the Bell, a free house that would once have been a canalside inn, for the Wilts & Berks ran under the lane here, though there was little to see of it now, and without close attention to the map as well as an interest in the canal, I would have missed it.

The old bridge over the Avon, and the lane from there into the village, gave fine views of Lacock Abbey; and my sister met me with a smile and no reproach for my half-hour of lateness. In the meantime she had identified a good place for lunch, and I was happy to adjourn immediately to the Carpenter's Arms, and enjoy steak and pigeon pie, washed down with Greene King IPA.

After lunch we walked around the familiar streets of the village – familiar because Lacock, being so well-preserved, has been used for any number of period dramas in both television and film: Emma, Pride & Prejudice, Cranford, Moll Flanders, the Mayor of Casterbridge, Robin Hood, Harry Potter, and many others have used Lacock in one way or another as a backdrop. As soon as the twenty-first century cars are cleared away, Lacock can look like a well-preserved 1930s village, or any period the film-makers want, right back to the middle ages; some of the buildings go back to the thirteenth century, and the way the stone-built houses blend together means that anachronisms hardly stand out. Betjeman praised this unity of atmosphere: 'they all fit in together: gabled cottages of the seventeenth century look perfectly at home beside the plainer houses of the nineteenth.'[1] This picturesque character can be preserved because the village has been owned by the National Trust since 1944.

We wandered down to the Bide Brook, the little stream that gives Lacock its name (*lacuc* being Saxon for small brook); and were lucky enough to spot a grass snake, hunting in the shallows on the far side of the brook. It was probably looking for frogs, and seemed more at home in water than on land.

Lacock was just a few houses and a couple of mills by this stream, until the coming of the abbey, after which charters were obtained for a weekly market and a three-day annual fair, and the village became a prosperous trading centre for wool. The market used to be held in front of St Cyriac's church, which we found well worth a look inside.

[1] Betjeman, 2009, *op cit*

I was impressed by the barrel-vaulted roof, and the large 'woolgothic' window above the chancel arch, letting in floods of daylight. Madge, as a clergy wife, noticed such things as the flowers and the individually embroidered hassocks, while I read about the six bells in the key of F, the oldest two dating from 1628, originally cast by Roger Purdue of Bristol. We had both already seen the abbey, but took the time to look round the Fox Talbot Museum, and learn more about the polymath pioneer photographer, who developed the positive-negative process, before adjourning to the Stables Tearooms.

Lacock Abbey was founded in the early thirteenth century as an Augustinian nunnery. Its first abbess was Ela, the widowed Countess of Salisbury, who founded the abbey one spring morning in 1232, and brought her late husband's heart to be buried here. He was William Longespée, one of the most distinguished of Henry II's several bastard sons. For centuries he was reputed to be the son of Fair Rosamund, but some 21st century research has found documentary evidence that his mother was in fact Ida de Tosny, a teenager under the protection of the king, who looked after her by making her his mistress for a while, before marrying her off to the Earl of Norfolk. Her son William grew up together with his half-brothers the princes, and later served Richard the Lion-heart on crusade, as well as being a close companion to King John,[1] who was more or less the same age, so they had probably been friends from early boyhood.

In 1196, twenty-year-old William Longespée was betrothed to nine-year-old Ela, effectively as a gift of a title from his royal half-brother Richard. Child betrothals, and child marriages, were commonplace amongst royalty and nobility at the time, usually for dynastic, political, or financial reasons, and the wishes of the children involved were irrelevant. However we have no reason to believe either party was unhappy; subsequent events would suggest that young Ela might have hero-worshipped the dashing young knight; and William might equally have been captivated by the sparky youngster, and looked forward to her adulthood.

The unequally-aged couple did not live together for several years afterwards; in any case William was mostly away, on crusade or engaged in other knightly activities. He bore the original Plantagenet arms, *Azure, six lions rampant Or, three, two, and one* – undifferenced, since his legitimate brothers used the royal lions passant.

[1] Given-Wilson, C & Curteis, A (1984) *The Royal Bastards of Medieval England* Routledge

The Countess was apparently devoted to her husband, refusing all offers of marriage when his death abroad was reported. He had been shipwrecked, and took many months to recover and find his way home; but Ela never believed that he was dead. Even when he did eventually die, and she was still less than forty years old, a strong and vigorous woman, she did not remarry, instead concentrating on her responsibilities as Countess of Salisbury, before 'retiring' to Lacock and the more constrained responsibilities of abbesshood.

She had had an eventful life; when she was very young, it is said that she was abducted by relatives and hidden somewhere in Normandy. They presumably hoped to profit by arranging a marriage to suit their interests. A knight from England, William Talbot, hunted down her hiding place by travelling as a troubadour from place to place. Romantic versions of the story have him singing outside the tower in which she was imprisoned; a more plausible version is that, having established her probable location through discreet inquiry, he gained employment with the family as a professional minstrel, which eventually gave him the opportunity to organise her escape.

In either case the language of the song, and the style of the music would have been French, still the first language of the aristocracy in England, and the only option in Normandy. The melody below, with its simple ground bass, is from the 13th century Montpellier Codex, and its liveliness might have appealed to a young girl.

The nuns at Lacock sang all the divine offices in French, a choice that was probably originally made by Abbess Ela; the founding nuns were mostly of noble birth, and Norman French would have been their mother tongue. The custom continued, however, long after French had ceased to be the language of the ruling class.

Twelve: Lacock to Bradford-on-Avon *(12 miles)*

Cattle hazard – mud – Madge's Maggot – toads to cure the plague – Conigre Mead – no way through – late lunch – Vortigern's fortress – Gudgeons from Snuffy

12th October 2012

Just after ten o'clock, I climbed out of my sister's car by the bridge over the Avon at Lacock, and set off across the fields, downriver towards Melksham, pausing only to take a photograph of the swollen river as it squeezed under the three low arches of the old bridge. The previous day had seen torrential rain, and the brown water surged close to the top of the riverbank, tugging at half-submerged bushes that would normally have stood at the water's edge.

Although no path was visible through the lush meadow grass, the galvanised metal gate on the far side of the field was very visible. I chose a slightly indirect curve towards it, to give a wide berth to the herd of dairy cattle. Only the day before, a woman had been trampled to death by a cow, just a couple of miles upriver from here; and the publicity had elicited reports of another case shortly before that, a few miles away, where the victim had survived, but with broken ribs and shoulder. In decades of country walking, I had not worried overmuch about cattle, other than bulls, but now, when one young heifer began to trot in my direction, I turned and told her to stop, which she did as long as I held her eye. If I took my eye off her, she started again, and two or three others also moved towards me. I was quite relieved to put the gate between myself and the herd.

I had anticipated mud and standing water in the meadows, and was wearing wellies accordingly; and before long I was glad of them. Each succeeding gate was surrounded by a semicircle of trampled brown mud, the deep hoofprints showing that cattle, rather than large numbers of ramblers, were responsible for the trampling. In some fields the softness and waterlogging were more widespread, and ordinary walking boots would have been almost submerged in places.

At one point I found that I was on the wrong side of a hedge that was bringing me too close to the river; but at a corner there was an old willow tree, whose low horizontal branches gave an opportunity to scramble over two fences and the ditch in between, into the next field from where I could rediscover the correct line of the right of way. A few hundred years ago, this would have been forest rather than farmland, the forest of Melksham, which was a northern continuation of the great forest of Selwood. The 17th century antiquary, John Aubrey, recorded its existence before his day: 'the forest of Milsham' he wrote, '...was full of goodly oakes, and so neer together that they say a squirrill might have leaped from tree to tree.'[1]

[1] Aubrey, J (1847) *Natural History of Wiltshire* Wiltshire Topographical Society

Now there was mainly grass, mud, and hedgerows, though the latter were decorated with many bright red haws and hips, as well as an abundant and unusually late crop of blackberries; I could have picked pounds of the sweet fruit, if I hadn't been walking to a deadline.

My sister would be waiting for me at the Old Bear in Staverton at one o'clock; three hours for six miles seemed manageable, but it didn't leave time for dawdling. I was very grateful for her ferrying and support, and had offered a specially-composed tune in her honour, to match whichever Playford dance was her favourite. She had chosen 'Orleans Baffled', one of my favourites too, and had then skipped around the room to check that the new tune matched the various turns and semi-poussettes of the dance. The hornpipe went round in my head now, as I progressed from field to field.

The last section of path to the outskirts of Melksham was across a ploughed field, the path itself well-trodden and glistening glutinously in the pale light of the sun ahead. Canine pawprints predominated over the skiddy prints of human footwear; clearly many dogs' need for exercise had prevailed on their owners to use this muddy route into the countryside.

On reaching suburbia, the path ran between hedges, with wide grassy verges where some of the mud could be walked off. This turned out to be the line of the old Wilts & Berks Canal, which had been turned into an urban walk. I passed the site of Melksham Forest Lock without realising it, and came to a playground with a quite remarkable number of notices outside, forbidding a wide range of activites and substances. One of the signposts identified the direction of the Canal Trail, and I followed this route further along a grassy embankment, then through an alley between back gardens, then a path with a hawthorn hedge on the right, through which could be glimpsed wild wasteland. I was on the former towpath, though the canal on the left had been absorbed by back gardens.

In the early years of the canal, the days of George IV and William IV, before the railways began to take all the freight, many heavy horses would have trodden this towpath, hauling barges laden with Somerset coal towards Abingdon. At first the Wilts & Berks was profitable, as noted by Cobbett:

> …we crossed *a canal* at a place where there is a wharf and a coal-yard, and close by these a gentleman's house, with coach-house, stables, walled-in garden, paddock *orné*, and the rest of those things, which, all together, make up *a villa*… When, upon further inquiry …I found that it was the villa of the chief manager, ['the *head un* o' the canal'], I could not help congratulating the proprietors of this aquatic concern; for …I could readily suppose, that the profits must be prodigious, when the residence of the manager would imply no disparagement of dignity, if occupied by a Secretary of State…[1]

At Murray Walk I turned right, since it looked as if it would lead me to the river, as indeed it did, passing over an overgrown backwater, dense with willows and rushes, until I came to the Avon itself, even broader and fuller than it had been three miles upstream. The riverside path led into King George V Park, where I spotted a small toad, immobile on the path, apparently basking in the sun.

Since the Wind in the Willows, toads have been regarded in a more positive light, as lovable eccentrics; but once they were seen as witches' familiars, embodiments of evil. On the other hand, they were also said to be a source of precious stones, though this may have been a metaphorical way of suggesting that they might have valuable properties. Medieval pictures nonetheless show toads being harvested for jewels.

Their poisonous secretions led to their being considered for medicinal uses, since many poisons can be of benefit if the right dosage can be established. Paracelsus suggested that the toad could be a cure for the plague:

> As to the other kind of plague which collects itself into a centrum (bubo), one should take toads well dried in the sun or in the air and put them straight on to the tumour. Then the toad swells up and attracts the plague poison through its whole skin, it grows large and full, and if it has filled up thus, it should be discarded and a fresh one should be put on.

But not everything (perhaps not very much) in Paracelsus is to be taken literally. His oblique references to the equivalence of toads and lilies are of heraldic/political rather than medicinal/philosophical significance. The ancient arms of France were *Azure semy of fleurs de lis Or*, with many small fleurs de lis strewn across the blue field. Some claimed that the little golden flowers had once been golden toads, the stylised forms of which eventually became the standard fleur de lis; and to support this theory it was asserted that the toad had been the personal symbol of Clovis the Great. True or not, Paracelsus uses the idea to indulge in a little anti-French insinuation:

[1] Cobbett, *op cit*

...but it should not be lilies but Toads. For a toad is the first given Magic Sign. But it is changed from a toad into a flower. For even as a toad inflates itself with poison, likewise does he inflate himself who is given to pride. It is not a garden lily but a lily growing out of thorns, that refuses to grant her fragrance to anyone.[1]

The little toad in Melksham was a light bronze colour that might almost have passed for gold in the sunlight. A passer-by, seeing me observing it, said that it ought to be returned to the river, since it would 'dry out' if separated from water. But the toad showed no sign of wishing to be anywhere other than where it was, so I left it crouching phlegmatically on the pathway, and walked on past the Melksham Gate. This was a large sluice on the far side of the river, which normally controls river levels in conjunction with a weir a few feet high.

Today there was no sign whatsoever of the weir; it must have been submerged by two feet or more, and the river was flowing past and through the gate at the same level, above and below. The Wilts & Berks Canal restoration scheme had a plan to construct a lock here, and use the river as a route through Melksham, since the original line of the canal had been too built over to restore. But no canal craft could safely navigate this river in conditions like today's. The water was high on the arches of the Town Bridge, and nothing bigger than a canoe could have passed through – even then the canoeist would have had to bend double. Further on, willow trees were standing in water that had risen to the level of the riverside walk, providing a couple of inches for the walker to wash his wellies in.

I was looking for Conigre Mead, somewhere ahead on this Riverside Walk, but the path was once again submerged by the overflowing river, this time to an unknown depth. I tried a couple of paces, trusting in the wellies, but it seemed to be descending too steeply, so I took a side path that led up to a cemetery, from where I found my way back down and into Conigre Mead, well equipped with new gates, paths and display panels, courtesy of a Lottery grant earlier in the year.

Tiny as it is, a triangle perhaps four hundred yards long and barely a hundred yards wide at its widest, Conigre Mead Nature Reserve has a variety of wildlife and is secluded and peaceful (if you can ignore the sound of the traffic on the nearby A350). I was impressed with tall pink flowers that were probably Musk Mallow, though I wondered if they were perhaps Bloody Cranesbill.

[1] Paracelsus, T (1536) *Prognostications*

The spindly stems and little yellow flowers of Hedge Mustard (or something similar), and the abundant foliage and drooping purple and white flowers of Comfrey were also noticeable; and the willow trees around the pond made an attractive picture.

Time was passing, however, and I left Conigre Mead by the main road entrance, and walked south along the verge as far as the signpost for the footpath to Staverton. I had an hour and twenty minutes for the next three miles, feasible if the going was good, but tight otherwise. Once over the stile, things looked challenging: a field recently ploughed and sown with some kind of brassica crop, tiny dark green leaves just showing above the soft damp earth. There was no indication of the line of the path, and I had to take a best guess at the diagonal from the map. It was heavy going, and I altered the angle slightly to pass through a gate into the meadow lower down. Although this was grass, it proved just as soft and heavy; in fact much more so in places, where streams were trickling down the slope, and ruts and bumps and hollows, and bovine hoofprints, retained the water and prevented drainage.

At the worst spot I found myself sinking to within an inch or two of the welly tops, extracting each boot in turn slowly and carefully so as not to leave one behind, and very relieved to reach slightly firmer ground – but then equally disappointed to find no feasible way out at the far end of the field. This meant the shortest way to Staverton was blocked, and I had to battle my way back past all the squelchiest places, and then take a line up the slope to farm buildings by Berryfield, to try and locate the next path.

A helpful farmer put me right, locating a concrete bridge over a ditch, which I hadn't spotted because it was obscured by dead branches of a fallen bush. It was obvious no rambler had been this way for some little time; but it was a right of way, and I knew where I was, though now my arrival in Staverton was likely to be rather late. The track or path ran straight on, keeping the houses of Berryfield on my left, until I came to the lane to Holbrook Farm. There should have been a continuation directly opposite, but none was to be seen; fifty yards to the east was a track leading across a plank bridge over a stream, where a Peacock butterfly added a spot of colour, and then a stile with a Wiltshire County Council waymarker reassured me that once more I was on the right path. However, over the stile was another newly-sown crop, and no path underfoot. A line of pylons a quarter of a mile ahead gave a clear idea of the right angle to take; but on the far side of the field was a fence and a deep ditch, with no visible way out. Following the fence all the way round the field brought me to the farmyard, and back to the lane.

Rather than further hunting for the elusive path, which might yet prove fruitless, it seemed the least unwise option would be to walk through Berryfield to the main road, down to the Kennet & Avon, and then from the canal to Staverton. This would be a mile and a half further than I'd bargained for, and together with the time I'd already lost, probably meant an hour's lateness at our rendezvous. I hoped my sister was in relaxed and forgiving mood, and set out at the best speed I could muster after the exertions so far.

The roads through Berryfield and Outmarsh, down to Semington Junction, turned out to be safe and quick walking, and the welcome rise in the road, indicating the presence of the Kennet & Avon, appeared sooner than I had feared. It was essential to press on, however, and I could only spare a quick glance at the site of the proposed junction with the restored Wilts & Berks, and another glance down to the Semington Brook, overflowing its banks under the aqueduct. The towpath here was stony, with little pointy ballast chips sticking up to tease tired feet. I discovered that half a dozen burdocks had attached themselves to my Turkish goathair pullover, and did my best to disentangle and extract them without slackening pace.

Several boats were on the move westwards, as I covered the two long miles to the Staverton Road, feet and legs complaining at the speed I was attempting, wondering what was positive about this last part of the walk. The usurped Duke, in *As You Like It*, works hard at making the best of his exile, optimistically saying 'Sweet are the uses of adversity, Which, like the toad, ugly and venomous, Wears yet a precious jewel in his head' – without knowing yet what the jewel might be. I was no more hopeful of a miraculously positive outcome than I would have been of extracting a diamond from the little golden toad in the park, and simply hoped that the Old Bear would not have finished serving lunch before I got there.

In this, at least, I was not disappointed, arriving at two and finding that last orders for lunch were at 2.15, while there were no sisterly reproaches for my hour's lateness. Pork and apple pie, and Ringwood best bitter, restored hydration and energy levels to some extent; and the firm decision was taken, since 'the destination of a Ramble is moveable',[1] to finish the day's walk, and this book, at Bradford-on-Avon, rather than the originally planned Avoncliffe.

The Old Bear was an attractive stone building, and around and opposite were other fine examples of stone architecture: Staverton had once been a prosperous weaving village. Madge gave me a lift back to the canal, and I resumed the walk at Hilperton Bridge, able to take the remaining couple of miles at a more relaxed pace, and with time to stop and take photographs of Hilperton Marina in its two large basins. These were originally busy wharves, offloading coal for Trowbridge, and loading local produce for transport to the cities. Now they were part of the leisure industry, and hire boats as well as privately owned craft lined both sides of the canal. A large crane was lifting a hire boat out of the water for a refit.

The towpath here was smoother, and it was pleasant to stroll and observe Red Admiral butterflies soaring over the water; or hips, haws, elderberries, and mauve hybrid cranesbill flowers brightening the hedgerow; or a passing narrowboat, solar panels propped up on the roof, 'For Sale' notices in the windows, proceeding westwards on a wobbly zigzag course as the steersman talked on his mobile. I was surprised to see *Nordic Fjord*, which I knew was a hire boat from Middlewich in Cheshire; either it had been hired for an unusually long period, maybe a month, to come as far south as this, or the fleet had sold it to a private owner.

[1] Harding, *op cit*

There was time to notice a cormorant flying overhead, or long-tailed tits twittering among the bushes below the embankment, as the canal ran close to the River Avon. Meadowsweet was still in flower on the far bank of the canal, and a long line of tall poplars had turned pale yellow, and caught the late afternoon sun as it filtered through. Fallen poplar leaves, yellow and pale and black, strewed the roof of another broad boat, peacefully moored and snug, with a wisp of smoke from its tall chimney.

I was saddened by the sight of *Chalfont*, neglected and forgotten, moss-grown timbers rotting as it leaned at a worrying angle, but correspondingly impressed by the smart broad boat *Moonraker*, as it passed Widbrook Marina, which had once been the entrance to the ill-fated Dorset & Somersetshire Canal. This had been proposed to link the Kennet & Avon to the River Stour in Dorset; it was begun in 1796, but abandoned in 1803 when the capital ran out, and never carried any traffic.

Soon I was approaching Bradford, and saw my sister coming towards me; we had intended to meet at the café run by the Kennet & Avon Canal Trust, but it was closed, and so I was left with memories of having enjoyed a pot of tea there in May, watching the boats ascending and descending Bradford Lock, the spot where the canal was begun in October 1794.

Bradford-on-Avon has been a significant place for more than a millennium and a half; Leland described it in the 16th century: 'The toune self of Bradeford stondith on the cliving of a slaty rokke, and hathe a meetly good market ons a weeke'.[1] It was apparently already fortified in the fifth century, for it seems likely to have been the 'Wirtgernesburg', where Cenwalh of the West Saxons won a victory; and the name means 'Vortigern's fortress'.[2]

Vortigern (right) was the warlord who was said to have been the first to invite Anglo-Saxon mercenaries to fight for him (Hengest and Horsa in 449), as he sought to extend his power from the territory of the Dobunni. The river Avon here was close to the southern edge of that territory, and would have been an obvious place to fortify; though no clear site for Vortigern's 'burg' has been identified.

[1] Toulmin Smith, *op cit*
[2] Laycock, *op cit*

More recently, probably in the 19th century, Bradford acquired the nickname of 'Snuffy'; some said because of the bargeloads of snuff that were hauled thither on the Kennet & Avon Canal. It is hardly likely that a small town could consume snuff by the bargeload; but the stimulant was manufactured in Devizes, and bargeloads would have passed this way en route to Bristol and the wider world. Another explanation is the smoggy atmosphere from the cloth industry, which flourished here before being undercut by cheaper products from Yorkshire.

If the town was 'Snuffy', the inhabitants were 'Gudgeons', from the fish on the weathervane of the little jail on the bridge. The fish is gilded and ornate, with a longer and finer dorsal fin than sported by a common gudgeon; but the Bradford Gudgeons took the name with pride, as the youths went off to do battle with the Trowbridge Knobs.

Just round a bend of the canal from the lock was the tithe barn, of a similar age to Great Coxwell's, and noticeably longer yet narrower, for here there were no pillars, and a simpler cruck construction of roof timbers resting directly on the walls, making it impossible to match the 44' width of Great Coxwell. The 168' length allowed for two transepts rather than one, so that the barn was distinctly different in style, yet similar in capacity and equally impressive to see.

As the tithe barn, and church, at Great Coxwell had provided a suitably ancient and atmospheric conclusion to the investigation of family roots, so the Bradford-on-Avon barn made a memorable ending to the Upper Thames and Wiltshire Ramble, a walk through thousands of years of English history.

Conclusion

Arrival in Bradford-on-Avon represented considerable progress towards the goals of the Four Points Ramble: 114 miles in this book, making a cumulative total of 533 miles in seven books on a continuous route from Arnside in Cumbria. Now I was into the South-West, which brought the Southernmost Point and Westernmost Point within reach, or so it felt, though there were still three books to be walked and written before either of those was under my boots.

I had completed the walk in just under a year, although it might well have been finished in seven months without the lateness of one train. Having to organise overnight stops in order to do a south of England walk from a home in Manchester proved an awkward constraint in the end, particularly on a limited budget, though it worked well enough in the early stages.

I had enjoyed the hospitality of sixteen pubs, lunching at some where food was available; and been frustrated by closed doors at others where I would have appreciated refreshment. For the best combination of excellent beer and tasty food, I would award first prize to the Barge at Honey Street, and second to the Plough at Kelmscott.

The literal high points of the walk had been Charlbury Hill at 790'; Giant's Grave at around 850'; Morgan's Hill at 860' or so, and highest of all, the shoulder of Tan Hill at 903', actually the highest point on the Four Points Ramble since the Cloud, on the Cheshire-Staffordshire border, about 300 miles ago. Among the high points in terms of enjoyment, satisfaction, awe, and wonder were the wide skies and open spaces of the Wansdyke; the tall trees of West Woods; the quiet beauty of the unspoilt Upper Thames; the company of the Vale of White Horse Ramblers; the privilege of playing for the Abingdon Morris Men; the man-made beauty of Oxford college architecture or Burne-Jones murals; the natural beauty of orange-tip butterflies on sunlit grass, or a robin's song on a light breeze - undeserved blessings, all of them.

There had been deeper layers of history to explore along this route than I had found in previous sections of the Ramble, and one theme running through the centuries had been undeserved Grace: all the way from the preaching of Germanus in the Dark Ages, through Wyclif, Colet, Tyndale, Latimer, Cranmer, Owen and Romaine to Tiptaft; from privileged nobility such as the Duchess of Gordon to obscure artisan Lollards like William Berford and William Wakeham.

I could only hope that the next section, Ramble through Somerset, would prove equally fascinating and instructive.

The Beneficiary Charities

On these two pages are details of the four charities that will benefit from the sale of this book.

Helen & Douglas House is a registered charity providing respite and end of life care for children and young adults with life-shortening conditions, as well as support and friendship for the whole family. The two hospice houses offer specialist symptom and pain management, medically-supported short breaks and end-of-life care. They are bright, vibrant and positive places, where the emphasis is on living life to the full, even when that life may be short.

There are currently around 300 families on the charity's books and they support over 60 bereaved families. It costs £4.5 million a year to run Helen & Douglas House, the majority of which comes from voluntary sources (i.e. not the government). Helen House opened in 1982 as the world's first children's hospice. Douglas House opened in 2004 as the world's first hospice specifically for young adults aged 16-35.

www.helenanddouglas.org.uk Registered Charity No: 1085951

The first Emmaus Community was founded in Paris in 1949 by Abbé Pierre, a priest, MP and former member of the French resistance. The idea spread around the world, but Emmaus didn't arrive in the UK until 1992, when the first Community opened in Cambridge.

Emmaus Communities enable people to move on from homelessness, providing work and a home in a supportive, family environment. Companions, as residents are known, work full time collecting renovating and reselling donated furniture. This work supports the Community financially and enables residents to develop skills, rebuild their self-respect and help others in greater need. Companions receive accommodation, food, clothing and a small weekly allowance, but for many, the greatest benefit is a fresh start. To join a Community, they sign off unemployment benefits and agree to participate in the life and work of the Community and abide by its rules, for example not bringing drugs or alcohol into the Community.

Emmaus is a secular movement, spanning 36 countries, with 19 Communities in the UK. Each Community aims to become self-supporting, with any surplus donated to others in need.

www.emmaus.org.uk Registered Charity No 1064470.

Together the Wildlife Trusts partnership manages over 2,200 nature reserves and has a membership of over 807,000 people. This makes us the largest UK network of organisations dedicated exclusively to conserving all our habitats and species. Our overall aim at The Wildlife Trusts is to achieve a UK richer in wildlife – for the benefit of all. We stand up for wildlife and want to inspire the nation about the nature on our doorsteps.

We aim to:

- inspire, encourage and support people to take action for wildlife
- buy, create and manage nature reserves to safeguard species and habitats
- work in partnership to conserve and enhance wildlife in the wider country-side and urban areas.

Whether you fancy getting into the great outdoors or being an armchair supporter, there are opportunities for all from volunteering and the chance to get some fresh air on one of our nature reserves, to taking part in one of the many events we run. Or perhaps leading one of our junior Wildlife Watch groups to inspire the next generation of naturalists. Your local Trust will be pleased to advise you about the opportunities on offer in your area.

www.wildlifetrusts.org Registered Charity No: 207238
For Wiltshire: www.wiltshirewildlife.org Registered Charity No: 266202

The Kennet & Avon Canal Trust aims to **'Protect, Enhance and Promote'** the canal. It is through this love and passion that the canal was restored to its current state. The volunteers were finally rewarded when the Queen opened the locks in 1990.

Today the Kennet and Avon is used by all from walkers to cyclists to boat enthusiasts.

We have five objectives:

- To support and increase Trust membership, canal volunteering and canal community networking:
- To protect, maintain and enhance the waterway through positive involvement and partnership with the Canal management, Local Government and others:
- To protect and enhance the waterway through fund raising, campaigning, funding and resource provision:
- To protect, enhance and promote the waterway and its story through the Trust museum, pumping stations, shops, boats and branch networks:
- To raise awareness of the canal and its potential.

www.katrust.org Registered Charity No: 209206

Bibliography

Abbott, CC ed (2ed 1956) *Further Letters of Gerard Manley Hopkins* OUP
Anderson, JRL & Godwin, F (1975) *The Oldest Road: an Exploration of the Ridgeway* Wildwood House
Andrews, CB ed (1934) *The Torrington Diaries* Eyre & Spottiswoode
Aubrey, J (1847) *Natural History of Wiltshire* Wiltshire Topographical Society
Auden, WH ed (1973) *Herbert: Poems and Prose* Penguin
Belloc, H (1907) *The Historic Thames* Dent
Betjeman, J (1938) *An Oxford University Chest* John Miles
Betjeman, J (2009) *Betjeman's England* John Murray
Bettey, JH (1986) *Wessex from AD 1000* Longman
Bewick, T (1826) *A History of British Birds*
Blair, PH (1956) *An Introduction to Anglo-Saxon England* CUP
Bliss, P (ed) (1857) *Reliquiae Hearnianae: The Remains of Thomas Hearne* Oxford
Briggs, A (1983) *A Social History of England* BCA
Buchan, J (1931) *The Blanket of the Dark* Hodder & Stoughton
Burne, AH (2002) *The Battlefields of England* Penguin
Carpenter, H (1978) *The Inklings: Lewis, Tolkien, Charles Williams and their Friends* Allen & Unwin
Chappell, W (1893) *Old English Popular Music* Chappell & Co
Chiang, Y (1944) *The Silent Traveller in Oxford* Methuen
Churchill, WS (1957) *A History of the English-Speaking Peoples* Cassell
Cobbett, W (1830) *Rural Rides*
Crisp, BW (1976) 'The towpath is for walking' *The Butty* No **72**
Crosley, GH (1976) 'The Devizes to Westminster Canoe Race', *The Butty* No **71**
Crossley, A et al eds (2007) *William Morris's Kelmscott: Landscape & History* Windgather
Culpeper, N (1653) *The Complete Herbal*
Cunliffe, B (1993) *Wessex to AD 1000* Longman
Cunliffe, B (1991) *Iron Age Communities in Britain* Routledge
d'Aubigné, JHM (1853) *The Reformation in England*
Esmonde Cleary, AS (1989) *The Ending of Roman Britain* Batsford
Forrest, J (1999) *The History of Morris Dancing 1458-1750* Univ Toronto Press
Foxe, J (1563) *Actes and Monuments of these Latter and Perillous Days*
Gardner, WH ed (1953) *Gerard Manley Hopkins* Penguin
Gasson, H (1976) *Footplate Days* Oxford Publishing Co
Gilpin, W (1786) *Observations, relative chiefly to Picturesque Beauty*
Gilpin, W (1794) *Three Essays on Picturesque Beauty*
Given-Wilson, C & Curteis, A (1984) *The Royal Bastards of Medieval England* Routledge
Golding, W (1967) *The Pyramid* Faber & Faber
Harding, M (1986) *Rambling On* Robson
Hibbert, C (1987) *The English: A Social History* Guild
Hippisley Cox, R (1914) *The Green Roads of England* Methuen
Hobson, MG (1962) *Oxford Council Acts* Clarendon
House, H ed (1959) *Journals & Papers of Gerard Manley Hopkins* OUP
Jefferies, R (1879) *Wildlife in a Southern County* Jonathan Cape
Jefferies, R (1880) *Hodge and His Masters* Smith, Elder & Co
Jubb, M (1980) *The Thames Valley Heritage Walk* Constable
Kennet DC (1977) 'The History of Devizes Wharf', *The Butty* No **75**
Laycock, S (2009) *Warlords: The Struggle for Power in Post-Roman Britain* History Press
Lewis CS (1991) *All My Road Before Me: Diary 1922-27* Harper Collins
Lewis, WH ed (1966) *Letters of CS Lewis* Harcourt Brace
Major, JF & Burrow, EJ (1926) *The Mystery of Wansdyke*
McDevitte, WA & Bohn, WS (1869) *Caesar's Gallic War*
Moody Stuart, Rev A (1865) *Life and Letters of Elizabeth, last Duchess of Gordon* J Nisbet

Morris, C ed (1982) *The Illustrated Journeys of Celia Fiennes* Webb & Bower
Morris, Rev FO (1850) *British Birds*
Morris, J (1978) *The Oxford Book of Oxford* OUP
Morris, W (1868) *The Earthly Paradise* Ellis
Morris, W (1882) *Hopes and Fears for Art* Ellis & White
Morris, W (1892) *News from Nowhere* Kelmscott Press
Nock, OS (1972) *GWR Steam* David & Charles
Owen, J (1684) *The Glory of Christ*
Paracelsus, T (1536) *Prognostications*
Payne, A et al (2006) *The Wessex Hillforts Project* English Heritage
Philpot, JH (1964) *The Seceders* Banner of Truth
Platt, C (1978) *Medieval England* Routledge Kegan Paul
Rashdall, H (1895) *Universities of Europe in the Middle Ages*
Rex, P (2007) *Edgar, King of the English 959-75* Tempus
Robinson, JA (1923) *The Times of St Dunstan* OUP
Robinson, M (2007) 'Environmental Archaeology & Historical Ecology of Kelmscott' in Crossley et al
Rodger, N (1997) *The Safeguard of the Sea: a Naval History of Britain* Harper Collins
Rowse, AL (1972) *The Elizabethan Renaissance* Macmillan
Ryle, JC (1885) *Christian Leaders of the 18th Century*
Saul, N & Given-Wilson, C (2002) *Fourteenth Century England vol 2* Boydell Press
Seebohm, F (1867) *The Oxford Reformers*
Smith, LT (1910) *The Itinerary of John Leland in or about the years 1535-43*
Sorley, CH (1915) *Marlborough, and other poems* CUP
Sorley, CH (ed Sorley, WR, 1919) *The Letters of Charles Sorley* CUP
Taunt, H (1875) *Illustrated Map of the Thames*
Thomas, E (1906) *The Heart of England* JM Dent & Sons
Thomas, E (1909) *The South Country* JM Dent & Sons
Thomson, J (1730) *The Seasons*
Thomson, JAF (1965) *The Later Lollards 1414-1520* OUP
Timperley, HW & Brill, E (1965) *Ancient Trackways of Wessex* Phoenix House
Tiptaft, W (2010) *Sermons of a Seceder* Gospel Standard Trust
Walsingham, T (ed Galbraith, V, 1937) *The St Albans Chronicle* Clarendon
Williams, A (1915) *Life in a Railway Factory* Duckworth & Co
Williams, A (1923) *Folk Songs of the Upper Thames* Duckworth & Co
Wood, M (2010) *The Story of England* Penguin
Yoon, S-H & Park, S (2011) 'A mechanical analysis of woodpecker drumming' *Bioinspiration and Biomimetics* **6**

Southwards and upwards